Real-Life English

A COMPETENCY–BASED ESL PROGRAM FOR ADULTS

Program Consultants

Jayme Adelson-Goldstein
North Hollywood Learning Center
North Hollywood, California

Patricia De Hesus-Lopez
Texas A & M University
Kingsville, Texas

Julia Collins
Los Angeles Unified School District
El Monte-Rosemead Adult School
El Monte, California

Federico Salas-Isnardi
Houston Community College
Adult Literacy Programs
Houston, Texas

Else V. Hamayan
Illinois Resource Center
Des Plaines, Illinois

Connie Villaruel
El Monte-Rosemead Adult School
El Monte, California

Kent Heitman
Carver Community Middle School
Delray Beach, Florida

Wei-hua (Wendy) Wen
Adult & Continuing Education
New York City Board of Education
New York, New York

STECK-VAUGHN
ELEMENTARY · SECONDARY · ADULT · LIBRARY

A Harcourt Company

www.steck-vaughn.com

information on this section, see "Evaluation" on page viii.

Placement

Any number of tests can be used to place students in the appropriate level of *Real-Life English*. The following tables indicate placement based on the CASAS and MELT (BEST Test) standards.

Student Performance Levels	CASAS Achievement Score	*Real-Life English*
	164 or under	Literacy
I	165–185	Level 1
II	186–190	
III	191–196	Level 2
IV	197–205	
V	206–210	Level 3
VI	211–216	
VII	217–225	Level 4
VIII	226 (+)	

Teaching Techniques

Presenting Chants

The chants can be used in a variety of ways. Students can learn to say the chants aloud, or they can listen to and/or read the chants and then answer questions about them. All the chants are recorded on the Audiocassettes. To present a chant, we suggest these steps:

♦ Play the tape or say the chant aloud one or two times as students listen. Establish a firm, steady beat by tapping your foot, clapping your hands, or snapping your fingers. Ask a few questions to make sure students understand. Clarify any words students need to know.

♦ Teach students the chant line-by-line. Say each line and have the class repeat chorally.

♦ Have the class say or read the chant chorally

while you take one of the parts.

♦ Divide the class into as many groups as there are parts in the chant, and have the groups say or read it chorally.

A number of techniques can be used to lend variety and excitement to the chants:

♦ Students might clap or tap out the rhythm as they say the chant. This will make the chant livelier and help students hear the rhythm better.

♦ Two or three students might act out the chant in front of the class as the rest of the class reads or says the chant.

♦ You might bring in (or have students bring in) simple props, costumes, and rhythm instruments.

Feel free to have the class say the chant throughout the rest of the unit. Students might enjoy saying the chant as a quick warm-up at the start of each class session.

Presenting Dialogs

To present a dialog, follow these suggested steps:

♦ Play the tape or say the dialog aloud two or more times. Ask one or two simple questions to make sure students understand.

♦ Say the dialog aloud line-by-line for students to repeat chorally, by rows, and then individually.

♦ Have students say or read the dialog together in pairs.

♦ Have several pairs say or read the dialog aloud for the class.

Reinforcing Vocabulary

To reinforce the words in the list on the Word Bank page, have students look over the list. Clarify any words they do not recognize. To provide additional reinforcement, use any of these techniques:

- **Vocabulary notebooks.** Have students use each new word to say a sentence for you to write on the board. Have students copy all of the sentences into their vocabulary notebooks.

- **Personal dictionaries.** Students can start personal dictionaries. For each new word students can write a simple definition and/or draw or glue in a picture of the object or the action.

- **Flash cards.** Flash cards are easy for you or for students to make. Write a new word or phrase on the front of each card. Provide a simple definition or a picture of the object or action on the back of the card. Students can use the cards to review vocabulary or to play a variety of games, such as Concentration.

- **The Remember-It Game.** Use this simple memory game to review vocabulary of every topic. For example, to reinforce food words, start the game by saying, *We're having a picnic, and we're going to bring apples.* The next student has to repeat the list and add an item. If someone cannot remember the whole list or cannot add a word, he or she has to drop out. The student who can remember the longest list wins.

Presenting Listening Activities

Use any of these suggestions:

- To activate students' prior knowledge, have them look at the illustrations, if any, and say as much as they can about them. Encourage them to make inferences about the content of the listening selection.

- Have students read the directions. To encourage them to focus their listening, have them read the questions so that they know exactly what to listen for.

- Play the tape or read the Listening Transcript aloud as students complete the activity. Rewind the tape and play it again as necessary.

- Check students' work.

In multi-task listenings, remind students that they will listen to the same passage several times and answer different questions each time. After students complete a section, check their work (or have students check their own or each others' work) before you rewind the tape and proceed to the next questions.

Prereading

To help students read the selections with ease and success, establish a purpose for reading and call on students' prior knowledge to make inferences about the reading. Use any of these techniques:

- Have students look over and describe any photographs, realia, and/or illustrations. Ask them to use the illustrations to say what they think the selection might be about.

- Have students read the title and any heads or sub-heads. Ask them what kind of information they think is in the selection and how it might be organized. Ask them where they might encounter such information outside of class and why they would want to read it.

- Have students read the questions that follow the selection to help them focus their reading. Ask them what kind of information they think they will find out when they read. Restate their ideas and/or write them on the board in acceptable English.

- Remind students that they do not have to know all the words in order to understand the selection. Then have students complete the activities on the page. Check their answers.

One To One

To use these information gap activities to maximum advantage, follow these steps:

- Put students in pairs, assign the roles of A and B, and have students turn to the appropriate pages. Make sure that students look only at their assigned pages.

- Present the dialog in Step 1. Follow the instructions in "Presenting Dialogs" on page vi. (Please note that as these conversations are intended to be models for free conversation, they are not recorded on the Audiocassettes.)

- When students can say the dialog with confidence, model Step 2 with a student. Remind students that they need to change the words in color to adapt the dialog in 1 to each new situation. Then have students complete the activity.

- Have students continue with the remaining steps on the page. For additional practice, make sure students switch roles (Student A becomes Student B and vice versa) and repeat Steps 2 and 3. When all students have completed all parts of both pages, check everyone's work, or have students check their own or each others' work.

Evaluation

To use the Check Your Competency pages successfully, follow these suggested procedures.

Before and during each evaluation, create a relaxed, affirming atmosphere. Chat with the students for a few minutes and review the material. When you and the students are ready, have students read the directions and look over each exercise before they complete it. If at any time you sense that students are becoming frustrated, stop to provide additional review. Resume when students are ready. The evaluation formats follow two basic patterns:

1. Speaking competencies are checked in the same two-part format used to present them in the unit. In the first part, a review, students fill in missing words in a brief conversation. In the second part, marked with the *Check Up* symbol, students' ability to use the competency is checked. Students use the dialog they have just completed as a model for their own conversations. As in the rest of the unit, color

indicates the words students change to talk about themselves. Follow these suggestions:

- When students are ready, have them complete the written portion. Check their answers. Then have students practice the dialog in pairs.

- Continue with the spoken part of the evaluation. Make sure that students remember that they are to substitute words about themselves for the words in color. Have students complete the spoken part in any or all of these ways:

Self- and Peer Evaluation: Have students complete the spoken activity in pairs. Students in each pair evaluate themselves and/or each other and report the results to you.

Teacher/Pair Evaluation: Have pairs complete the activity as you observe. Begin with the most proficient students. As other students who are ready to be evaluated wait, have them practice in pairs. Students who complete the evaluation successfully can peer-teach those who are waiting or those who need additional review.

Teacher/Individual Evaluation: Have individuals complete the activity with you as partner. Follow the procedures in Teacher/Pair Evaluation.

2. Listening, reading, and **writing** competencies are checked in a simple one-step process. When students are ready to begin, have them read the instructions. Demonstrate the first item and have students complete the activity. Then check their work. If necessary, provide any review needed, and have students try the activity again.

When students demonstrate mastery of a competency to your satisfaction, have them record their success by checking the appropriate box at the top of the Student Book page. The Teacher's Edition also contains charts for you to reproduce and use to keep track of individual and class progress.

Real-Life English

1 Personal Communication

What are the people doing? What are they saying? What do you think?

Listen and practice the chant.

Hi!
Hello!
How do you do?
What's your name?
How are you?

My first name is Marta.
My last name is Cantu.
I'm from Nicaragua.
How about you?

Starting Out

A. Practice the dialog.

> ➤ Where are you from, **Mei?**
> ● I'm from **China.** I'm **Chinese.**
> ➤ What language do you speak?
> ● I speak **Chinese.**
> ➤ Where do you live?
> ● **San Francisco, California.** How about you?

B. Complete the sentences. Write about yourself.

1. I'm from _____ .
   (country)

2. I'm _____ .
   (nationality)

3. I speak _____ .
   (language)

4. I live in _____ .
   (city, state)

C. Work with a partner.
Use the dialog in A to talk about yourself.

Talk It Over

A. Practice the dialog.

➤ Hi. I'm a new student in your class.

● Hello. My name's **Ana Smith.** What's your name?

➤ **Pablo Bueno.**

● How do you spell that?

➤ My first name is **Pablo, P-A-B-L-O.** My last name is **Bueno, B-U-E-N-O.**

● Where are you from, **Pablo?**

➤ **Mexico.** I'm **Mexican.**

● What language do you speak?

➤ I speak **Spanish.**

● Nice to meet you, **Pablo.**

➤ Nice to meet you, too, **Ms. Smith.**

**B. Talk to three students.
Use the dialog in A.
Write the answers.**

	First Name	Last Name	Country	Nationality	Language
Example	Pablo	Bueno	Mexico	Mexican	Spanish
Student 1					
Student 2					
Student 3					

Word Bank

A. Study the vocabulary.

0	zero	name
1	one	first name
2	two	middle name
3	three	last name
4	four	address
5	five	city
6	six	state
7	seven	ZIP Code
8	eight	Social Security number
9	nine	area code
10	ten	telephone number

Useful Language

Where do you live?

What language do you speak?

How do you spell that?

How about you?

Binh Do
567 Fourth Street
New York, NY 10167

Maria Garcia
123 First Street
Los Angeles, CA 91251

STUDENT IDENTIFICATION CARD
Maria Garcia
Print Name
562-74-9031
Social Security Number
Mexico
Native Country
123 First Street
Address
Los Angeles, CA 91251
Maria Garcia
Signature

SOCIAL SECURITY
562-74-9031
THIS NUMBER HAS BEEN ESTABLISHED FOR
MARIA GARCIA
Maria Garcia
SIGNATURE

B. Complete the dialog. Use words from A.

➤ What's your _____address_____?
● **123 First Street.**

➤ What _____ and state do you live in?
● **Los Angeles, California.**

➤ What's your ZIP _____?
● **91251.**

➤ What's your telephone number, _____ code first?
● **(818) 230-2143.**

➤ What _____ do you speak?
● **Spanish.**

About You ## C. Work with a partner
Use the dialog in B to talk about yourself.

Listening

A. Look, listen, and complete the name.

1. <u>M</u> E __ __
2. __ __MI __H
3. __A __ L __ S
4. __AB __O

B. Look, listen, and write the area code.

1. Chicago _<u>312</u>_
2. New York City _____
3. Miami _____
4. Washington, D.C. _____

C. Look, listen, and write the number.

1. ZIP Code _____60657_____

2. Area code _____

3. Telephone number _____

4. Social Security number _____

D. Look, listen, and complete the form.

APPLICATION
CITY LEARNING CENTER
ENGLISH PROGRAM

cLc

Name: _____Martinka_____
      (FIRST)   (LAST)

Address: _____Lake Street_____
         (NUMBER AND STREET)   (APT.)

         Miami   Florida
         (CITY)   (STATE)   (ZIP CODE)

Telephone: _____
           (AREA CODE)   (NUMBER)

Language: _____Russian_____

Social Security Number: _____

Reading

A. Look and read.

CITY LEARNING CENTER BULLETIN
New Students

Pedro Mendoza and Sylvia Li are new students in Level 1.
Pedro Mendoza lives in Miami, Florida.
He's from Puerto Rico.
His address is 820 School Street.
His ZIP Code is 33152.

Sylvia Li is from China.
She lives in Miami, Florida, too.
Her address is 345 Green Street.
Her ZIP Code is 33187.

B. Answer the questions about Pedro and Sylvia.

e	1. What's his ZIP Code?	a.	Li
___	2. What's her last name?	b.	Mendoza
___	3. Where do they live?	c.	345 Green Street
___	4. What's his last name?	d.	Miami, Florida
___	5. What's her address?	✔ e.	33152

C. Complete the sentences about Pedro and Sylvia.

1. Pedro and Sylvia live in _____ Miami, Florida _____.

2. His _____ is 820 School Street.

3. Her ZIP Code is _____.

4. _____ is a city in Florida.

Structure Base

A. Study the examples.

I am		a new student.
He	is	
She		

We		are new students.
You		
They		

B. Complete the sentences. Use the words from A.

1. Tuyet is my friend. _____She is_____ from Vietnam.

2. I am Tron. _____ from Vietnam, too.

3. Tuyet and I are in Level 1. _____ new students.

4. Chen and Jiang are in the class, too. _____ from China.

5. Pablo is a new student. _____ from Mexico.

C. Work with a partner.
Use the sentences in B to talk about the students in your class.

About You

D. Study the examples.

I	+	am	=	I'm
he	+	is	=	he's
she	+	is	=	she's

we	+	are	=	we're
you	+	are	=	you're
they	+	are	=	they're

E. Change the words. Use the new words from D.

1. **She is** from Vietnam.   _She's_ from Vietnam.

2. **I am** from Vietnam, too.   _____ from Vietnam, too.

3. **We are** in Level 1.   _____ in Level 1.

4. **They are** from China.   _____ from China.

5. **He is** from Mexico.   _____ from Mexico.

F. Study the examples.

I	my
he	his
she	her
we	our
you	your
they	their

My last name is Bueno.

G. Work with a small group.
Introduce yourself. Use the words from F. Say everyone's name.

My name is Elena.
Her name is Sylvia.
His name is Chris.

H. Study the examples.

Where are	you	from?
	they	
Where's	she	
	he	

I'm	from Korea.
She's	
He's	
We're	
They're	

I. Work with a partner.
Use the sentences in H to talk about the students in your class.

➤ Where's she from?
● She's from Mexico.

Write It Down

A. Study the names.

Print your name. _____ Pablo Bueno _____

Sign your name. _____ *Pablo Bueno* _____
(Signature)

B. Write your name.

Print your name. _____

Sign your name. _____
(Signature)

About You

C. Complete the form.
Write about yourself.

SEATTLE LIBRARY

APPLICATION FOR CARD

PLEASE PRINT.

Name: _____
(LAST)   (FIRST)   (MIDDLE)

Address: _____
(NUMBER AND STREET)   (APT.)

_____
(CITY)

_____
(STATE)   (ZIP CODE)

Telephone: _____
(AREA CODE)   (NUMBER)

Social Security Number: _____

Signature: _____

One To One

Student A

I. Practice the dialog.

> What's **his** name?
● **Kai Wong.**
> How do you spell that?
● **His** first name is **K-A-I. His** last name is **W-O-N-G.**
> Where does **he** live?
● **New Jersey.**
> Where's **he** from?
● **China.**

2. Who are they? Ask Student B. Follow the dialog in I. Write the information.

1. <u>Kai Wong</u>　　2. _____　　3. _____

　<u>New Jersey</u>　　　_____　　　_____

　<u>China</u>　　　　　_____　　　_____

3. Who are they? Tell Student B. Follow the dialog in I.

4. Steve Jones　　5. Maria Garcia　　6. Binh Do

　Ohio　　　　　　California　　　　New York

　Illinois　　　　　Texas　　　　　　Vietnam

Unit 1　　　　　　　　　　　　　　　　　　　　　　11

One To One

Student B

I. Practice the dialog.

➤ What's **his** name?
● **Kai Wong.**
➤ How do you spell that?
● **His** first name is **K-A-I. His** last name is **W-O-N-G.**
➤ Where does **he** live?
● **New Jersey.**
➤ Where's **he** from?
● **China.**

2. Who are they? Tell Student A. Follow the dialog in I.

1. Kai Wong
   New Jersey
   China

2. Sylvia Cho
   Florida
   China

3. Pedro Mendoza
   Florida
   Puerto Rico

3. Who are they? Ask Student A. Follow the dialog in I. Write the information.

About You

4. Steve Jones
   Ohio
   Illinois

5. _____

6. _____

Extension

 A. Practice the dialog.

> ➤ Hello. I'm **Sandy Ryan.**
> ● Nice to meet you, **Sandy.** I'm **Toma Matesa.**
> ➤ Good to meet you, too, **Toma.** Where are you from?
> ● I'm from **Poland.** Are you from **Minnesota?**
> ➤ Yes. Do you live in **Minnesota?**
> ● Yes. I'm a new student.
> ➤ Well, welcome to school.
> ● Thanks.

About You **B. Work with a partner.**
Use the dialog in A to talk about yourself.

 C. Practice the dialog.

> ➤ Hello, **Toma.**
> ● Hi, **Sandy.** How are you?
> ➤ Fine, thanks. How about you?
> ● Fine, thanks.
> ➤ How do you like **Minnesota?**
> ● I really like it.
> ➤ Well, good to see you, **Toma.**
> ● Thanks, **Sandy.** Nice to see you, too.

About You **D. Work with a partner.**
Follow the dialog in C.
Talk about yourself.

Can you use the competencies?

☐ 1. Ask for and give personal information
☐ 2. Say hello
☐ 3. Introduce yourself
☐ 4. Complete an identification form

A. Review competencies 1 and 2. Complete the dialog.

✔

| address   area   first   from   name   number   security |

➤ Hello, I need an identification card.

● OK. What's your ___first___ name and last ___name___?
➤ **Elena Martinka.**

● What's your ___address___?
➤ **3440 Lake Street, Miami, Florida 33153.**

● Your ___area___ code and telephone ___number___?
➤ **(305) 555-1987.**

● Where are you ___from___?
➤ **Russia.**

● What's your Social ___security___ number?
➤ **281-39-1011.**

Use competencies 1 and 2.
Use the dialog above to talk about yourself.

B. Review competencies 2 and 3. Complete the dialog.

✔

| hello   hi   your   name |

➤ _Hello_ . I'm a new student.

● _hi_ . My name's **Sylvia.** What's _your_ name?

➤ My _name_ is **Pedro.**

● Good to meet you.

➤ Good to meet you, too.

Check Up

Use competencies 2 and 3.
Use the dialog above to talk about yourself.

Check Up

C. Use competency 4.
Complete the form.

APPLICATION for IDENTIFICATION CARD

Name: _Villagran_ _Agustin_
          LAST   FIRST

Nationality: _mexico_

Social Security Number: _____

Address: _124   s san lorenso_ _#6_
           NUMBER   STREET   APT.

_____
        CITY   STATE   ZIP CODE

Phone: _____
        AREA CODE   PHONE NUMBER

Unit
2 Our Community

Unit Competencies

1. Identify places
2. Tell where places are
3. Read maps
4. Ask for, give, and follow directions
5. Use a pay phone to report an emergency

Where are the people? What are they saying? What do you think?

Listen and practice the chant.

Where are you going?
Do you know the way?

I'm going to the supermarket
on Park Street today.

Which way is it?
Do you know how far?

Go left on this street.
It's not very far.

The bank is on fire!
What can we do?

Call the fire department!
Call an ambulance, too!

Starting Out

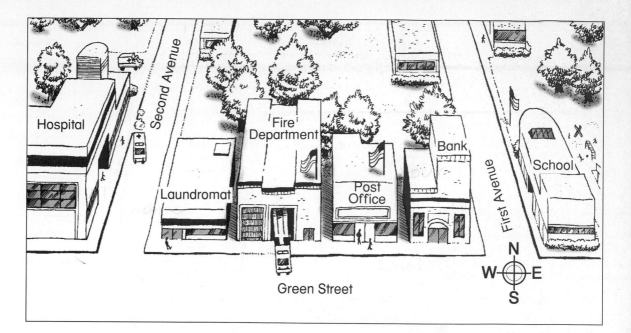

A. Practice the dialog.

- ➤ Where's the **bank?**
- ● It's next to the **post office.**
- ➤ Is it **between** the **laundromat** and the **post office?**
- ● No, it isn't. It's **on the corner of First Avenue and Green Street.**
- ➤ Is the **bank across from the school?**
- ● Yes, it is.

B. Complete the sentences. Use the map in A.

1. The laundromat is next to the _____fire department_____.

2. The fire department is between the laundromat and the

   _____post office_____.

3. The _____Hospital_____ is across from the laundromat.

4. The _____Bank_____ is on First Avenue.

C. Work with a partner.
Where do you want to go?
Use the dialog in A to talk about places on the map.

Talk It Over

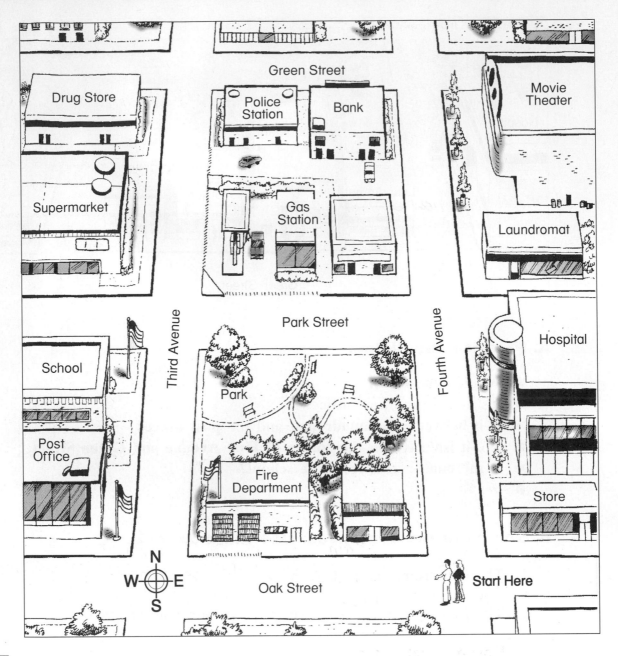

A. Practice the dialog.

➤ Excuse me. Where's the **police station?**
● It's **one block** north of the **park.**
➤ Where?
● **One block north** of the **park,** on **Green Street.**
➤ **One block north** of the **park,** on **Green Street.** Thanks.

About You

B. Work with a partner.
Where do you want to go?
Use the dialog in A to ask for directions
to places on the map.

Word Bank

A. Study the vocabulary.

Places   store
bank   supermarket
drug store
fire department   accident
gas station   fire
hospital
laundromat   ambulance
movie theater   fire truck
park   police car   north   block
police station   south   corner
post office   left   east
school   right   west

Useful Language
Go (north).
Turn (right).
How do I get (there)?
There's a (fire).

B. Complete the dialog.
Use the map on page 18. Use words from A.

➤ How do I get to the **bank** from here?

● Go **two blocks** _____north_____ on **Fourth** _____Avenue_____.

Turn ___left___ on **Green Street.**

The **bank** is **on the** ___corner___ of **Fourth Avenue and Green Street.**

C. Work with a partner.
Where do you want to go?
Use the dialog in B to ask for directions to places on the map on page 18.

Listening

About You **A. Look, listen, and write the places on the map.** ✔

bank hospital post office store

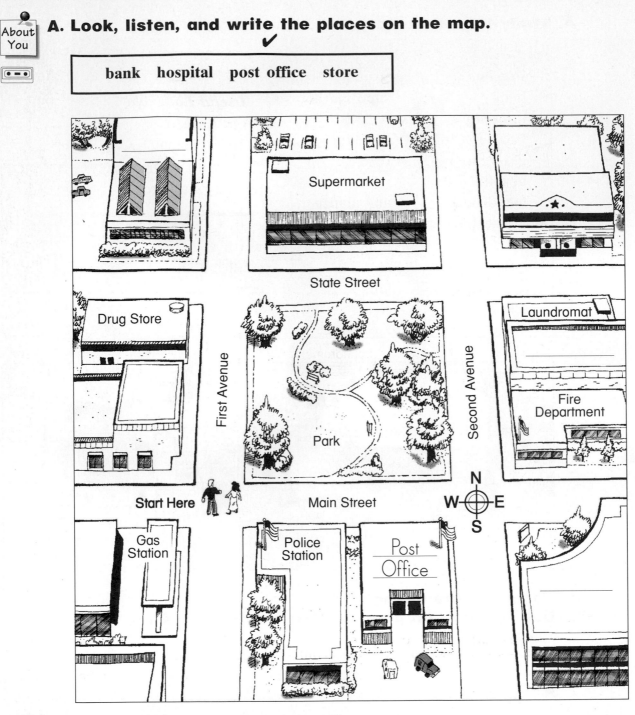

About You **B. Look, listen, and follow the directions.**
Draw a line on the map.

About You **C. Where do you want to go?**
Ask a partner for directions.
Draw a line on the map.

Reading

A. Look and read.

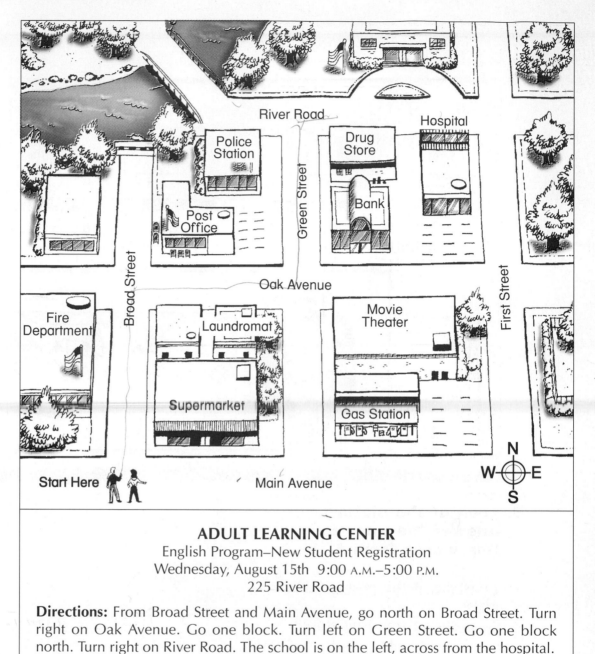

ADULT LEARNING CENTER
English Program–New Student Registration
Wednesday, August 15th 9:00 A.M.–5:00 P.M.
225 River Road

Directions: From Broad Street and Main Avenue, go north on Broad Street. Turn right on Oak Avenue. Go one block. Turn left on Green Street. Go one block north. Turn right on River Road. The school is on the left, across from the hospital.

B. Answer the questions.

1. What can you study at the Adult Learning Center? _____

2. What's the address of the Adult Learning Center? _____

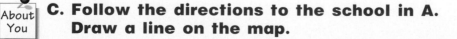

About You **C. Follow the directions to the school in A.**
Draw a line on the map.

Structure Base

A. Study the examples.

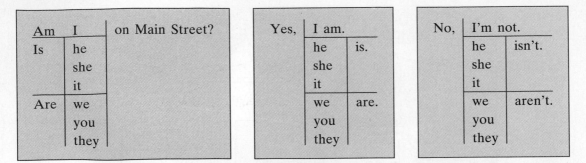

Am	I	on Main Street?
Is	he	
	she	
	it	
Are	we	
	you	
	they	

Yes,	I am.	
	he	is.
	she	
	it	
	we	are.
	you	
	they	

No,	I'm not.	
	he	isn't.
	she	
	it	
	we	aren't.
	you	
	they	

**B. Look at the picture.
Answer the questions.
Use words from A.**

1. Is she at the post office? _No, she isn't._

2. Is she at the drug store? no she isn't.

3. Is she at the store? yes she is

4. Is the store on Park Street? no it isn't.

5. Is the store on Oak Avenue? yes it itys

C. Study the examples.

The fire department is	on Main Street.
	on the corner of Main and Oak.
	next to the police station.
	between the police station and the school.
	across from the movie theater.

D. Work with a small group.
Use the sentences in C to talk about places in your city or town.

E. Study the example.

Where's the fire department?

F. Work with a partner.
Talk about places in your city or town.

➤ Where's the **drug store?**
● It's **on First Avenue.**
➤ Is it **next to the movie theater?**
● **Yes, it is.**

G. Study the examples.

an	accident
	emergency

a	hospital
	police car

H. Complete the sentences. Write *a* or *an.*

➤ Oh, no! __An__ accident! Call __an__ ambulance.

● Yes, call __a__ fire truck, too.

★ OK. Where's __a__ phone?

Write It Down

A. Look at the map.
Complete the directions to the school.

Turn ___right___ on Oak Avenue. Go ___one___ block north.

Turn left on ___maple street___. The school is on the ___left___.

It's next to the ___Drug Store___. It's across from the ___Gas station___.

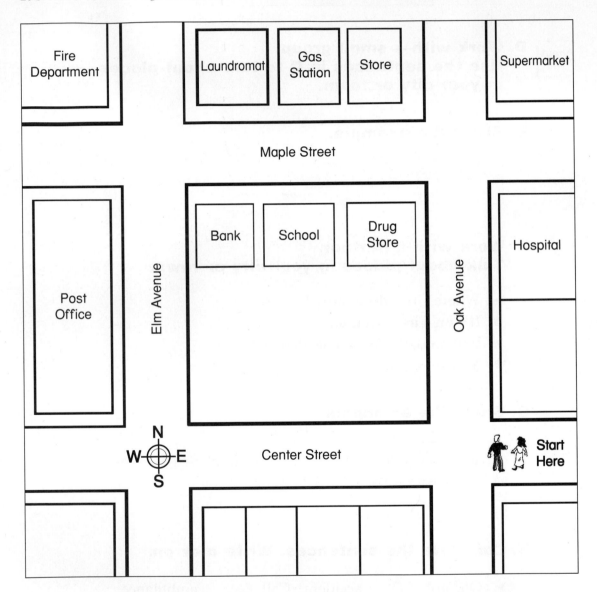

B. Make a map of your neighborhood on a sheet of paper.
Where do you live?
Where do you want to go?
Write directions under the map.

I. Practice the dialog.

➤ Excuse me. Where's the **fire department?**

● It's **north of the post office.**

➤ Where?

● **North of the post office.**
It's **on First Avenue, across from the bank.**

➤ **On First Avenue, across from the bank.** Thanks.

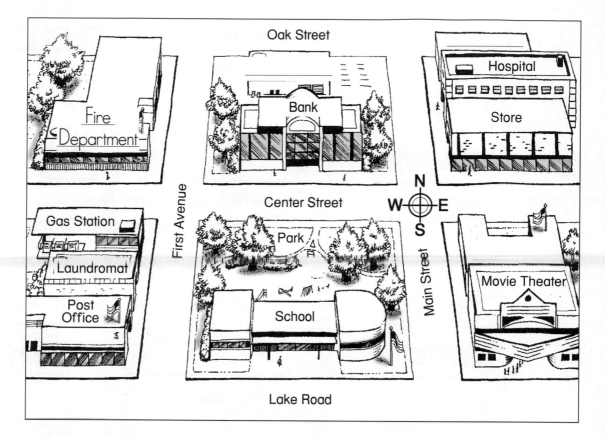

About You

2. Ask Student B for directions. Follow the dialog in I. Write the places on the map.

the fire department
the police station
the supermarket
the drug store

About You

3. Give Student B directions.
Use the map. Follow the dialog in I.

4. Switch roles. Turn to page 26. Complete 2 and 3.

I. Practice the dialog.

➤ Excuse me. Where's the **fire department?**

● It's **north of the post office.**

➤ Where?

● **North of the post office.**
  It's **on First Avenue, across from the bank.**

➤ **On First Avenue, across from the bank.** Thanks.

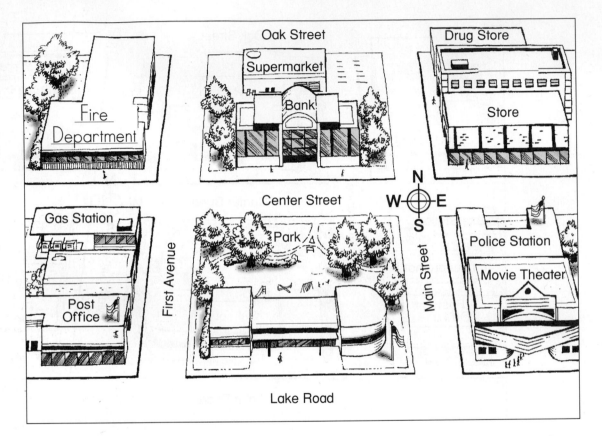

**2. Give Student A directions.
   Use the map. Follow the dialog in I.**

**3. Ask Student A for directions. Follow the dialog in I.
   Write the places on the map.**

   the hospital
   the laundromat
   the school

4. Switch roles. Turn to page 25. Complete 2 and 3.

Extension

A. Practice the dialog.

➤ Oh, no! An accident!
  Find a telephone.
● OK.

➤ Pick up the telephone.
  Dial 911.
  Say that there's an accident.

★ Parkview, Lake County 911.
● There's an accident.
  Please send an ambulance.

★ Where's the accident?
● 410 Green Street.
★ OK. We'll be right there.

B. Work with a partner.
Use the dialog in A to report other emergencies.

Can you use the competencies?

- ☐ 1. Identify places
- ☐ 2. Tell where places are
- ☐ 3. Read maps
- ☐ 4. Ask for, give, and follow directions
- ☐ 5. Use a pay phone to report an emergency

Check Up

A. Use competency I. Look at the pictures. Circle the name of the place.

1. (laundromat)

   park

2. post office

   gas station

3. fire department

   movie theater

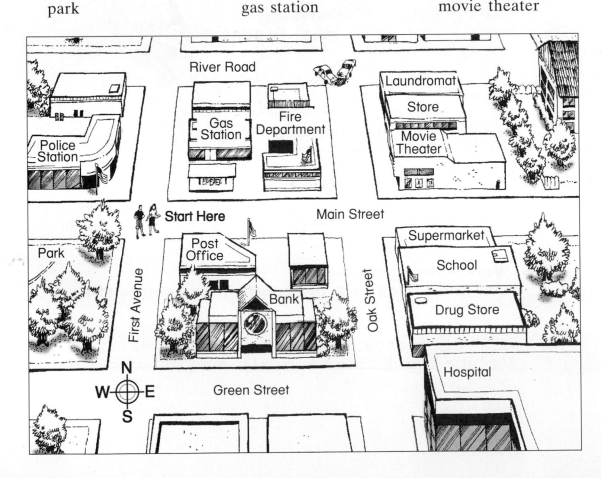

**B. Review competencies 2, 3, and 4. Complete the dialog.
Use the map on page 28.**

✔

block   east   left   next to

➤ Excuse me. Where's the **store?**

● Go **one block** _____east_____ on **Main Street.** Turn

_____. Go **one** _____ **north** on **Oak Street.**

The **store** is _____ the **movie theater.**

➤ OK. Thanks.

Check Up

**Use competencies 2, 3, and 4.
Use the dialog in B to give directions
to another place on the map on page 28.**

Check Up

**C. Use competency 4.
Listen to the directions.
Draw a line on the map on page 28.**

D. Review competency 5. Complete the dialog.

✔

accident   ambulance   telephone   911

➤ There's **an accident!** Find a ____telephone____. Dial _____.

● **Fairview, Lake County 911.**

➤ There's **an** _____ at **River Road and Oak Street.**

Send **an** _____.

Check Up

**Use competency 5.
Use the dialog above to report another emergency.**

3 School and Country

Unit Competencies

1. Listen for room numbers
2. Identify people and places at school
3. Talk about where places are in buildings
4. Read building directories
5. Write absentee notes

Where are the people? What are they saying? What do you think?

🔊 **Listen and practice the chant.**

How old is he?
What class is he in?

He's six years old.
His name is Minh.

Are you his mother?

Yes, I am.

Fill out the form.
My name is Pam.
Then go and meet
his teacher Kay.
Welcome to school.
Have a nice day.

Starting Out

A. Look, listen, and read.

In the U.S. all children have to go to school starting at age 6.
Today is Anh Luc's first day in school.

1. Anh's talking to his teacher.

2. Alma and Chen are opening the windows.

3. Sarita's sharpening pencils.

4. Binh, Alma, and Miguel are reading. Jesse's writing.

About You

B. Answer the questions.

1. What are the children doing?
2. Is this school like the schools in your country?
   Explain.

Talk It Over

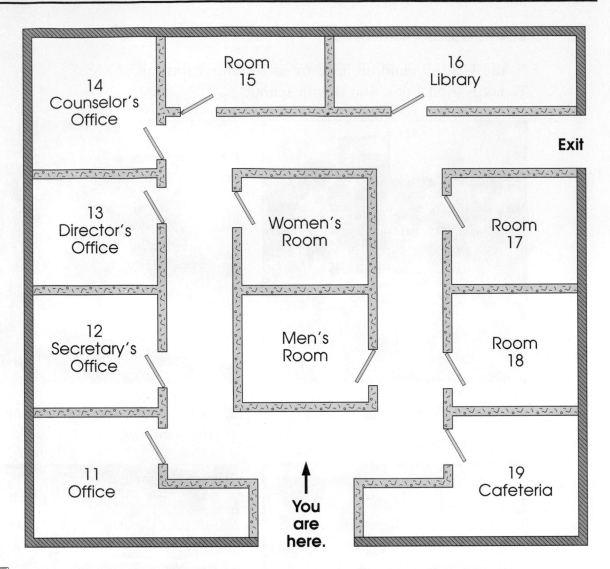

A. Today is Miguel Soto's first day at City Learning Center. Practice the dialog.

➤ Excuse me. Where's the **director's office?**
● Room **13.**
➤ Room **13?**
● Yes, **13.**
➤ How do I get there?
● Go **left.** Go **around the corner** and **down the hall.** It's on the **left.**
➤ Thanks.
● You're welcome.

B. Work with a partner.
Where do you want to go?
Use the dialog in A to talk about places on the map.

Word Bank

A. Study the vocabulary.

```
11 eleven
12 twelve
13 thirteen
14 fourteen
15 fifteen
16 sixteen        door            counselor
17 seventeen      exit            director
18 eighteen                       secretary
19 nineteen       board           student
20 twenty         book            teacher
30 thirty         desk
40 forty          eraser          close
50 fifty          notebook        erase
60 sixty          paper           open
70 seventy        pen             read
80 eighty         pencil          write
90 ninety
100 one hundred
```

cafeteria
room
library
office
men's room
women's room

EXIT

Useful Language
Excuse me.
It's around the corner.
It's down the hall.
You're welcome.

**B. Look at the map on page 32. Complete the dialog.
Use words from the list in A.**

➤ Where's the **director's** office?

● Room _____. Turn _____. Go

_____ the corner.

➤ Thanks.

**C. Work with a partner.
Use the dialog in B to talk about places in your school.**

Listening

A. Look, listen, and write the room numbers.

1. Level 1 English   ___11___

2. Level 2 English   _____

3. Level 3 English   _____

4. Level 4 English   _____

B. Look, listen, and write the room numbers on the map.

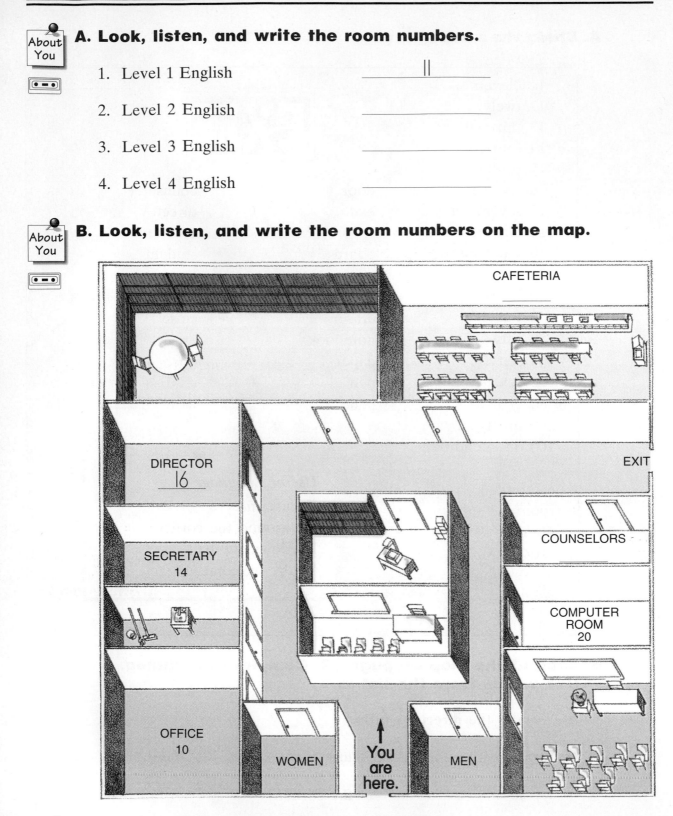

C. Look, listen, and follow the directions.
Draw a line on the map.

Reading

A. Look and read.

```
LINCOLN HIGH SCHOOL
14327 CRENSHAW
LOS ANGELES, CA 94194
213-555-7963


NAME:    Gerardo Monte
GRADE:   9
ADDRESS: 32231 Wilton
         Los Angeles, CA 94191
```

Class	Teacher	Grade	Comments
English	Ms. J. Burgess	A	Gerardo is doing great work!
U.S. History	Mr. L. Rizzo	C	Gerardo's work is getting better. He's reading more. He needs to speak more in class.
Math	Mr. A. Wen	B	Gerardo is working hard at math and doing well now.
Advanced Spanish	Ms. M. Iglesias	A	Gerardo is doing very well this year.

A = Excellent   **B** = Very good   **C** = Average   **D** = Below average   **F** = Failing

B. Answer the questions about Gerardo Monte's grade report.

1. How many A's did he get? _2_

2. How many B's did he get? _____

3. How many C's did he get? _____

C. Work with a partner. Answer the questions.

1. Which classes is Gerardo doing well in?
2. Does he need to study more in math?
3. Gerardo's mother wants to talk to his English teacher. What's her name?
4. Do you think Gerardo's a good student?
5. Do you have children? How are their grades?

Unit 3

35

Structure Base

A. Study the examples.

I'm	reading a book.
He's	
She's	
We're	
You're	
They're	

I'm not		reading a book.
He	isn't	
She		
We	aren't	
You		
They		

B. Write the correct form of the word.

1. Mei's meeting _____ (meet) the teacher.

2. The students _____ (not talking).

   They _____ (study).

3. Arnulfo and Lee _____ (sharpen) their pencils.

4. David _____ (close) the window.

5. Mei _____ (not read) a book.

   She _____ (read) a magazine.

C. Study the examples.

Am I		doing good work?
Is	he	
	she	
Are	we	
	you	
	they	

Yes,	you	are.
No,		aren't.

What	are you	doing?
Where		going?

D. Miguel and Sylvia are talking on the telephone. Complete the dialog. Use the patterns in A and C.

➤ What _____are_____ you _____doing_____ (do)?

● I'm _____ (study).

➤ What _____ you _____ (study)?

● English.

➤ _____ you _____ (read)?

● No, I'm not. _____ (write).

E. Work with a small group. Use the patterns in A and C to talk about the students in your class.

F. Study the examples.

the student's book   the students' books

G. Write the word. Use 's or s'.

➤ I'm going to the _____counselors'_____ (counselors) office.

● Where is it?

➤ It's next to the _____ (director) office.

● Oh. Thanks.

Write It Down

A. Look and read.

Alma's sick.
She's staying home from school.
Ms. Vargas is writing a note to Alma's teacher.

B. Complete the note.

✔

| excuse   home   school   sick |

> Dear Mr. Reyna,
>
>   Alma is __sick__ today, Tuesday, January 12.
>
>   She's staying _____ from _____.
>
>   Please _____ her.
>
>   Thank you very much.
>
>   *Ms. Vargas*

About You

C. You're sick.
You're not going to English class today.
Write a note to your teacher on a sheet of paper.

I. Practice the dialog.

➤ Excuse me. Where's the **library?**

● **Go down the hall. Turn left. The library's on the right.**

➤ OK. Thanks.

● You're welcome.

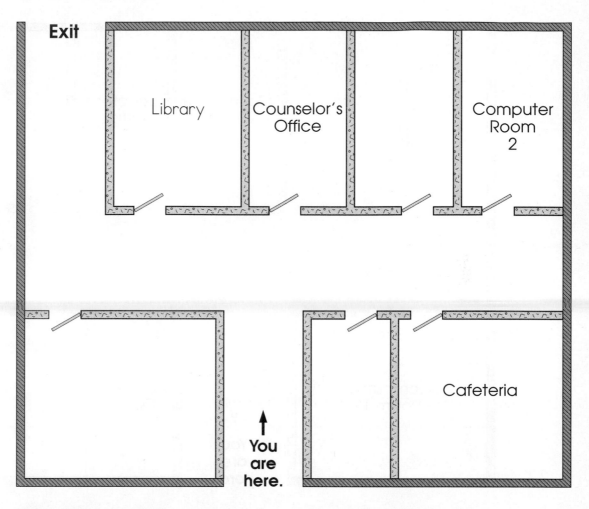

2. Ask Student B for directions. Follow the dialog in I. Write the places on the map.

the library
the director's office
computer room 1
the secretary's office

3. Give Student B directions. Use the map. Follow the dialog in I.

4. Switch roles. Turn to page 40. Complete 2 and 3.

I. Practice the dialog.

➤ Excuse me. Where's the **library?**
● **Go down the hall. Turn left. The library's on the right.**
➤ OK. Thanks.
● You're welcome.

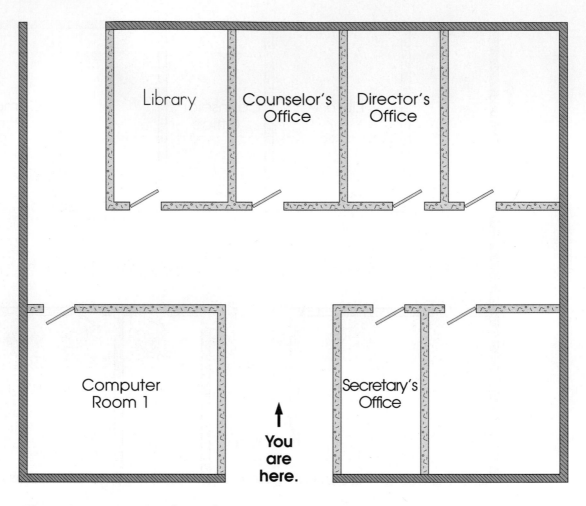

2. Give Student A directions. Use the map.
   Follow the dialog in I.

3. Ask Student A for directions. Follow the dialog in I.
   Write the places on the map.

computer room 2
the cafeteria
the exit

4. Switch roles. Turn to page 39. Complete 2 and 3.

Extension

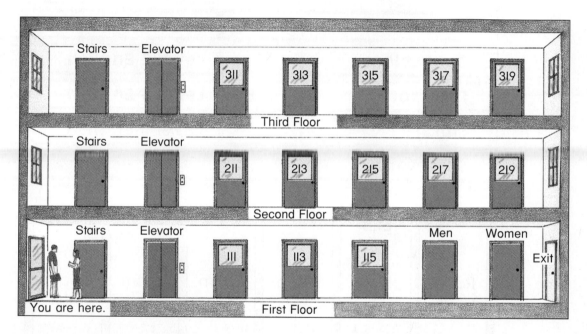

Adult English Center Building Directory

Cafeteria ············· 115	Library ··················· 113
Counselors ··········· 213	Office ···················· 111
English	Director ··············· 217
Level 1 ············· 317	Secretary ············· 215
Level 2 ············· 315	
Level 3 ············· 313	**Restrooms are located**
Level 4 ············· 311	**on the first floor.**

A. Look at the building directory and the map.

Stairs — Elevator — 311 — 313 — 315 — 317 — 319 — Third Floor

Stairs — Elevator — 211 — 213 — 215 — 217 — 219 — Second Floor

Stairs — Elevator — 111 — 113 — 115 — Men — Women — Exit

You are here. — First Floor

B. Practice the dialog.

➤ Excuse me. Where's the **Level 1 English class?**

● On the **third floor**, room **317.**

➤ How do I get there?

● **Go up the stairs or take the elevator to the third floor.**
   Then go down the hall.

➤ OK. Thanks.

● You're welcome.

C. Work with a partner.

About You

Use the building directory and the map.
Where do you want to go? Use the dialog in B.

Check Your Competency

Can you use the competencies?

☐ 1. Listen for room numbers
☐ 2. Identify people and places at school
☐ 3. Talk about where places are in buildings
☐ 4. Read building directories
☐ 5. Write absentee notes

Check Up

A. Use competency I. Listen.
Write the room numbers on the building directory.

Building Directory			
Cafeteria	120	Level 1 English	
Counselors	117	Level 2 English	113
Director	118	Level 3 English	114
Library		Level 4 English	115
Secretary			

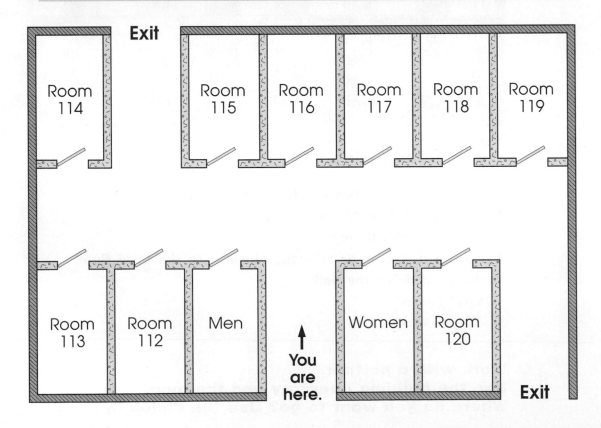

42   Unit 3

B. Review competencies 2, 3, and 4.
   Use the building directory and the map. Complete the dialog.

✔

| left   office   right   room |

➤ Excuse me. Where's the **director's** _____office_____ ?

● _____ **118.**

➤ Where's that?

● Go down the hall. **Turn** _____. The **director's office** is

   on the _____.

Check Up — **Use competencies 2, 3, and 4. Follow the dialog in B.**
Talk about other places on the map.

Check Up — **C. Use competency 5. Complete the note.**

| excuse   school   sick |

Dear _____,
(your teacher's name)
I'm _sick_ today.

I'm staying home from _____.

Please _____ me.

Thank you very much.

_____
(your signature)

4 Daily Living

Where are the people? What are they saying? What do you think?

Listen and practice the chant.

Get up! Wake up!
You sleepyhead!
    I can't wake up.
Get out of bed!
    What time is it?
It's time to go.
    Do I have to get up?
    It's raining, you know.
It's the first day of fall.
    What's the date?
September twenty-first.
    Oh no! I'm late!
    I have to be on time today.
Hurry up! Get on your way!

Starting Out

A. Look, listen, and read.

1. It's January 3. It's winter.
It's a cold night.
It's snowing. It's very windy.
She's driving home.

2. It's April 9. It's spring.
It's a warm morning.
It's raining.
She's walking to work.

3. It's July 19. It's summer.
It's a hot afternoon.
It's very sunny.
He's cutting the grass at work.

4. It's October 30. It's fall.
It's a cool morning.
It's cloudy.
They're going to school.

B. Work with a partner. Answer the questions.

1. It's summer. How's the weather?
2. It's winter. How's the weather?
3. It's spring. How's the weather?

C. Work with a partner. Use the sentences in A to talk about the weather today. What are people doing?

Talk It Over

A. Listen and practice the dialogs.

➤ What time is it?
● It's **two o'clock.**
➤ **Two o'clock?**
● Yes.
➤ Thanks.

➤ What time is it?
● It's **three-thirty.**
➤ Excuse me?
● **Three-thirty.**
➤ Thanks.

 B. Write the times.

12:00

 **C. Work with a partner. Follow one of the dialogs in A.
Say the times in B.**

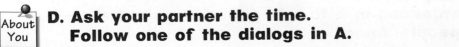 **D. Ask your partner the time.
Follow one of the dialogs in A.**

Word Bank

A. Study the vocabulary.

1st	first
2nd	second
3rd	third
4th	fourth
5th	fifth
6th	sixth

Useful Language

How's the weather?

What's your date of birth?

7th	seventh	17th	seventeenth
8th	eighth	18th	eighteenth
9th	ninth	19th	nineteenth
10th	tenth	20th	twentieth
11th	eleventh	21st	twenty-first
12th	twelfth	30th	thirtieth
13th	thirteenth	31st	thirty-first
14th	fourteenth		
15th	fifteenth	morning	
16th	sixteenth	afternoon	
		night	

Day

Sunday
Monday
Tuesday
Wednesday
Thursday
Friday
Saturday

Seasons	Winter	Spring	Summer	Fall
Months	December January February	March April May	June July August	September October November
Weather	hot warm sunny	cool cloudy windy		cold snowing raining

B. Look and read.

We write: _____ July 12, 1994 _____.

We say: _____ July twelfth, nineteen ninety-four _____.

C. Work with a partner. Say the dates.

1. November 2, 1995
2. July 13, 1997
3. February 23, 1996
4. October 31, 1994

Listening

About You

A. Look, listen, and write the time.

1. _____9:00_____

2. _____

3. _____

4. _____

About You

B. Look, listen, and circle the date.

1. (June 7)   June 17   June 27

2. October 6   October 16   October 26

3. April 9   April 19   April 29

About You

**C. Look and listen to the weather forecast.
Write the number of the forecast on the line.**

_____   _____

Reading

A. Read the holiday schedule.

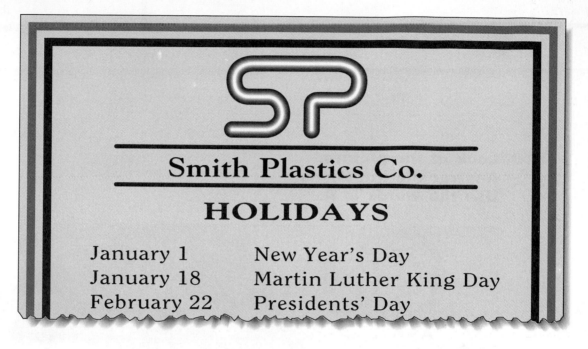

B. Circle the holidays on the calendar pages.

January						
S	M	T	W	T	F	S
					①	2
3	4	5	6	7	8	9
10	11	12	13	14	15	16
17	18	19	20	21	22	23
24/31	25	26	27	28	29	30

February						
S	M	T	W	T	F	S
	1	2	3	4	5	6
7	8	9	10	11	12	13
14	15	16	17	18	19	20
21	22	23	24	25	26	27
28						

About You

C. Complete the sentences about the calendar pages.

1. What day is January 1?   It's _____.

2. What day is January 18?   It's _____.

3. What day is February 22?   It's _____.

About You

D. Work with a partner.
What holidays are coming up? When are they?

Structure Base

A. Study the examples.

What	month day season time	is it?

It's	May. Tuesday. spring. 10:00.

B. Look at the picture.
Answer the questions.
Use the words in A.

1. What month is it?   It's April.

2. What day is it?   _____

3. What time is it?   _____

C. Study the examples.

It's	raining. snowing.

It's	sunny. cold. windy. cool. hot.

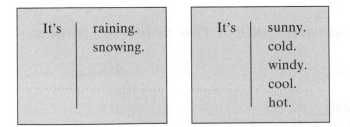

D. Work with a partner.
Talk about the time, the date, and the weather.
Use the words in A and C.

E. Study the examples.

Is it	snowing? cold? January? winter? sunny? Saturday?

Yes, No,	it	is. isn't.

F. Look at the picture.
Complete the sentences.
Use the words from E.

1. _____Is it_____ **December?**   No, ____it isn't____.

2. _____ **January?**   Yes, _____.

3. _____ **warm?**   No, _____.

4. _____ **cold?**   Yes, _____.

5. _____ **snowing?**   Yes, _____.

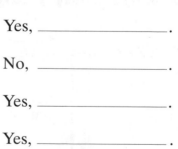

About You

G. Work with a partner.
Talk about the weather today.
Follow the sentences in F.

Write It Down

A. Kwan's date of birth is April 12, 1970.
He wrote his date of birth on the form.
Look and read.

```
___4_/_12_/70___
Date of birth

_Kwan Sun_____     ___/___/___
Signature              Date
```

B. Study the chart.

1	=	January	7	=	July	55 =	1955
2	=	February	8	=	August	60 =	1960
3	=	March	9	=	September	65 =	1965
4	=	April	10	=	October	70 =	1970
5	=	May	11	=	November	71 =	1971
6	=	June	12	=	December	72 =	1972

C. Write today's date on the form in A.

About You

D. Write today's date and your date of birth on the form.

```
___/___/___
Date of birth

_____     ___/___/___
Signature              Date
```

52 Unit 4

l. Practice the dialog.

➤ Excuse me. What's the **date?**
● **November 27.**
➤ What **time** is it?
● It's **4:30.**
➤ Excuse me?
● **4:30.**

 2. Ask Student B for the time and the date.
Follow the dialog in l. Write the information.

a.   November 27

         4:30

b. _____

_____

c. _____

_____

3. Give Student B the time and the date. Follow the dialog in l.

a.

December						
S	M	T	W	TH	F	S
					1	2	3
4	5	6	7	8	9	10
11	12	13	14	15	16	17
18	19	20	21	22	23	24
25	26	27	28	29	30	31

b.

February
23

c.

May						
S	M	T	W	TH	F	S
	1	2	3	4	5	6
7	8	9	10	11	12	13
14	15	16	17	18	19	20
21	22	23	24	25	26	27
28	29	30	31			

4. Switch roles. Turn to page 54. Complete 2 and 3.

I. Practice the dialog.

➤ Excuse me. What's the **date?**

● **November 27.**

➤ What **time** is it?

● It's **4:30.**

➤ Excuse me?

● **4:30.**

2. Give Student A the time and the date. Follow the dialog in I.

a.

	November					
S	M	T	W	TH	F	S
		1	2	3	4	5
6	7	8	9	10	11	12
13	14	15	16	17	18	19
20	21	22	23	24	25	26
(27)	28	29	30			

b.

January
15

c.

	September					
S	M	T	W	TH	F	S
1	2	3	4	5	6	7
8	9	10	11	12	13	14
15	16	17	18	19	(20)	21
22	23	24	25	26	27	28
29	30					

2:00

3. Ask Student A for the time and the date. Follow the dialog in I. Write the information.

a. ___December 12___

___4:30___

b. _____

_____

c. _____

_____

4. Switch roles. Turn to page 53. Complete 2 and 3.

Extension

BANK HOURS
MONDAY–FRIDAY 8:00–5:00
SATURDAY   9:00–12:00

We will close at 3:00
on New Year's Eve.
We will reopen
Saturday, January 2.
Happy New Year!

A. Practice the dialog.

➤ Are you open tomorrow?

● Yes. But we close early. It's New Year's Eve.

➤ What about Friday?

● It's New Year's Day. We're closed all day.

➤ When do you open?

● On Saturday.

➤ What are the hours?

● 9 o'clock to 12 noon.

About You B. Work with a partner. Answer the questions.

1. What time does the bank close on New Year's Eve?
2. Is the bank open on Friday?
3. What time does the bank open on Saturday?

Can you use the competencies?

☐ 1. Talk about seasons and weather
☐ 2. Ask for, say, and write times and dates
☐ 3. Read calendars
☐ 4. Listen for times and dates
☐ 5. Listen to weather forecasts
☐ 6. Read store hour signs

**A. Review competency 1.
Complete the dialog.**

✔

cold   isn't   windy

➤ How's the weather?

● It's winter. It's ___cold___. It's _____. It _____ snowing.

**Use competency 1.
Use the dialog above to talk about the weather today.**

B. Review competency 2. Complete the dialog.

✔

date   January 10   me   time

➤ Excuse _____me_____. What's today's _____?

● It's _____.

➤ What _____ is it?

● It's **4:00.**

**Use competency 2.
Use the dialog above to talk about today.
Then write the time and the date.**

Today is _____.

It's _____.

C. Use competency 3.
Use the calendar.
Answer the questions.

NOVEMBER						
S	M	T	W	T	F	S
	1	2	3	4	5	6
7	8	9	10	11	12	13
14	15	16	17	18	19	20
21	22	23	24	25	26	27
28	29	30				

1. What day is November 1?   It's _____Monday_____.

2. What day is November 14?   It's _____.

3. What day is November 26?   It's _____.

D. Use competencies 4 and 5.
Listen to the radio weather report.
Circle the time, the date, and the weather.

1. What time is it?   7:30   (8:30)   9:30

2. What's the date?   **January 14**   **July 14**   **June 14**

3. What day is it?   **Saturday**   **Sunday**   **Monday**

4. What's the weather like?   **warm**   **cool**   **sunny**   **cloudy**

E. Use competency 6. Read the sign.
Write _yes_ or _no_.

1. It's 8:30 Saturday morning. Is the bank open?   No

2. It's 8:30 Monday morning. Is the bank open?   _____

3. It's 1:00 Friday afternoon. Is the bank open?   _____

TOWN BANK
HOURS
Monday–Friday 8:00 A.M. to 5:00 P.M.
Saturday 9:00 A.M. to 1:00 P.M.

Unit 4   57

Food

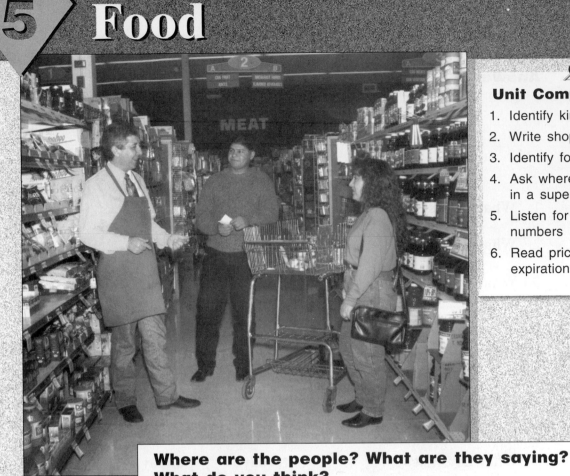

Unit Competencies

1. Identify kinds of food
2. Write shopping lists
3. Identify food packaging
4. Ask where things are in a supermarket
5. Listen for aisle numbers
6. Read price tags and expiration dates

Where are the people? What are they saying? What do you think?

🔊 **Listen and practice the chant.**

Excuse me, please, I'm looking for tea.

It's on the top shelf in aisle three.

What else do we need?

A gallon of milk, two pounds of steak,
A loaf of bread, and a chocolate cake.

Anything else?

Some corn and beans, and strawberry jam.

Ready to check out?

Yes, I am.

Starting Out

A. Practice the dialogs.

➤ Excuse me. I want **carrots** and a **watermelon.** Where's the fruit and vegetable section?
● Aisle 1.

➤ I want **some bread.** Where's the bakery?
● Aisle 2.

➤ I want **a half gallon of milk** and **a dozen eggs.** Where's the dairy section?
● Aisle 3.

➤ I want **two pounds of chicken** and **a pound of ground beef.** Where's the meat section?
● Aisle 4.

B. Work with a partner.
Use the dialogs in A to ask where you can find the food.

1. cheese
2. potatoes
3. steak
4. lettuce
5. apples

Talk It Over

 A. Practice the dialog.

> ➤ What do we want from the grocery store, Bill?
> ● **Apples, oranges, and bananas.**
> ➤ Anything else?
> ● **Some cheese.**
> ➤ How much?
> ● About **half a pound.**
> ➤ Is that all?
> ● No. Let's get **a bottle of oil and a loaf of bread,** too.
> ➤ OK.

B. Work with three other students.
Talk about what they want from the grocery store.
Write the answers.

Name	Food

Word Bank

A. Study the vocabulary.

Fruit
apples
bananas
grapes
oranges
tomatoes
watermelon

Useful Language
What do you want?
I want (bananas).

onions   candy
potatoes   oil
                rice

Meat
chicken
fish   **Dairy Products**
ground beef   butter   a half gallon
pork   cheese   a gallon
steak   eggs   a half pound
                milk   a pound
                                a dozen

Vegetables   **Bakery**   a loaf (of bread)
beans   bread
carrots   cake   cents
lettuce   cookies   dollar

B. Look at the pictures. What are they?
   Where do you find them? Write the section.

Food	Section
grapes	fruit and vegetable

C. Work with a partner. Look at the food in B.
   What do you want? Write a list of food on a sheet of paper.
   Write the sections where you find them.

Listening

A. What are the people looking for?
Look, listen, and circle the letter in column A.

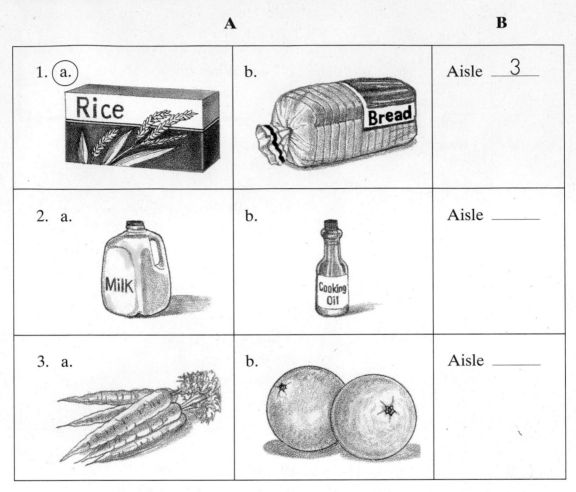

	A		B
1. (a.) Rice	b. Bread		Aisle _3_
2. a. Milk	b. Cooking Oil		Aisle _____
3. a.	b.		Aisle _____

Listen again and write the aisle number in column B.

B. Look, listen, and circle the food the people want to buy.

butter   cake   (ground beef)   lettuce   milk

onions   pepper   potatoes   tomatoes   eggs

C. Listen. Look at the food you circled in B.
Check off the groceries they bought.
Then answer the questions.

1. What did they forget?   _____cake_____

2. What extra item did Francisco buy?   _____

Reading

A. Look and read.

Many food packages have expiration dates.
Before the date, the food is good.
After the date, the food is bad.
Today's date is 9/22/94. Is the food good or bad?
Circle the expiration dates of the good food.

1.
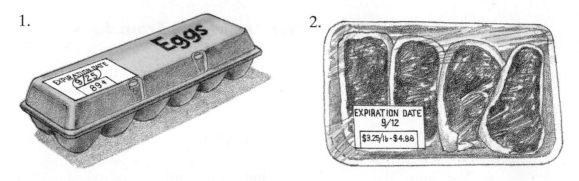

EXPIRATION DATE
9/25
89¢

2.

EXPIRATION DATE
9/12
$3.25/lb - $4.88

3.
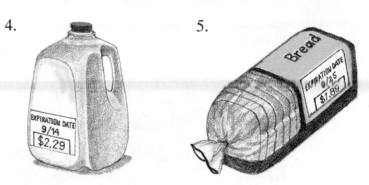

EXPIRATION DATE
9/30
$2.25

4.

EXPIRATION DATE
9/14
$2.29

5.

EXPIRATION DATE
9/25
$1.89

About You

B. You bought the eggs, the cheese, and the bread. Is the receipt correct? Circle the mistake.

Food Fair Market

Thanks for shopping at
Food Fair !

cheese	$ 2.25
eggs	.99
bread	1.89

Structure Base

A. Study the examples.

I want	a	potato.
	an	egg.
	some	eggs.
		potatoes.

I want some	lettuce.
	water.

B. Complete the dialog. Use the words from A.

➤ What do we need to make breakfast?

● _____Some_____ eggs and _____ potato.

➤ We need _____ onion and _____ bread, too.

● Yes, and _____ milk. Oh, and _____ butter.

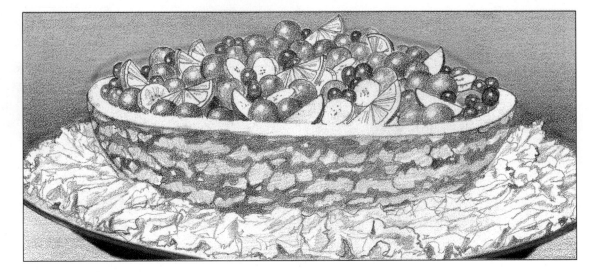

C. Complete the dialog. Write *a, an,* or *some.*

➤ Let's make fruit salad.

● OK. I'll write __a__ shopping list.

➤ Buy _____ grapes and _____ orange. Buy

_____ apple and _____ banana.

● What about _____ watermelon?

➤ Good idea. Buy _____ lettuce, too.

D. Study the examples.

How	much	lettuce water	do you want?
	many	eggs potatoes	

E. Bill's writing Jennifer's shopping list.
Read the answers. Write the questions.

➤ <u>How many potatoes do you want?</u>

● I want **8 potatoes.**

➤ _____

● I want **a pound of cheese.**

➤ _____

● I want **7 bananas.**

➤ _____

● I want **2 pounds of ground beef.**

F. Work with a partner.
Use the language in E to talk about food you want.
Write your partner's list.

SHOPPING LIST

Write It Down

A. Here are meals for one day.
Look at the pictures.

Breakfast   Lunch   Dinner

Write a shopping list for the meals in the pictures.

Shopping List

eggs _____   _____

_____   _____

_____   _____

_____   _____

_____   _____

_____   _____

_____   _____

About You **B. What do you want for breakfast, lunch, and dinner?**
Write your shopping list on a sheet of paper.

l. Practice the dialog.

> ➤ How much are **eggs** at **Food World?**
> ● **89 cents.**

**2. You want to know the prices at Food World.
Student B has the ad.
Ask Student B. Follow the dialog in l.
Write the prices.**

broccoli   _59¢_

eggs   _____

milk   _____

tomatoes   _____

**3. Student B wants to know the prices at Food Mart.
Use this ad. Follow the dialog in l.**

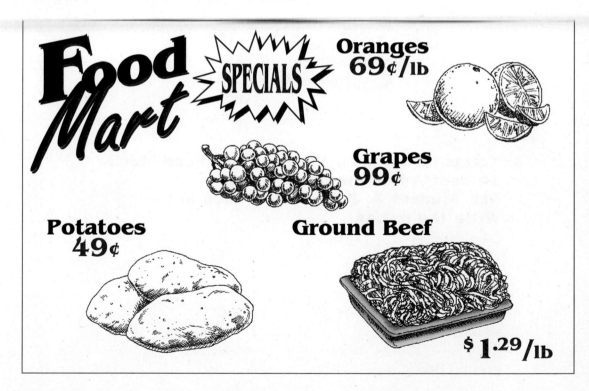

4. Switch roles. Turn to page 68. Complete 2 and 3.

I. **Practice the dialog.**

> ➤ How much are **eggs** at **Food World**?
> ● **89 cents.**

2. **Student A wants to know the prices at Food World.**
   Use this ad. Follow the dialog in I.

MILK

$1.79

On Sale at **FOOD WORLD**

59¢

TOMATOES

FRESH BROCCOLI

59¢

89¢

EGGS

3. **You want to know the prices at Food Mart.**
   Student A has the ad.
   Ask Student A. Follow the dialog in I.
   Write the prices.

grapes   _____99¢_____

potatoes   _____

oranges   _____

ground beef   _____

4. **Switch roles. Turn to page 67. Complete 2 and 3.**

Extension

 A. Look at the food. Which do you eat?

B. Look at the food. How is the food packaged?
Read the words.

1. box   2. bag   3. jar   4. carton   5. bottle

 C. How is the food in A and B packaged?
Write the package.

1. a _____ box _____ of cereal

2. a _____ of honey

3. a _____ of soy sauce

4. a _____ of sugar

5. a _____ of milk

Unit 5

69

Can you use the competencies?

☐ 1. Identify kinds of food
☐ 2. Write shopping lists
☐ 3. Identify food packaging
☐ 4. Ask where things are in a supermarket
☐ 5. Listen for aisle numbers
☐ 6. Read price tags and expiration dates

Check Up **A. Use competencies 1 and 2.
Look at the pictures.
Write a shopping list.**

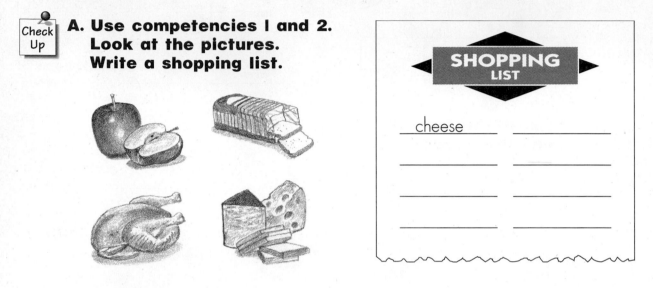

SHOPPING LIST

cheese _____   _____

_____   _____

_____   _____

_____   _____

Check Up **B. Use competency 3. Look at the pictures. Circle the package.**

1. box   2. box   3. box
   (carton)   bag   jar

4. bag   5. carton
   jar   bag

C. Review competencies. Complete the dialog.

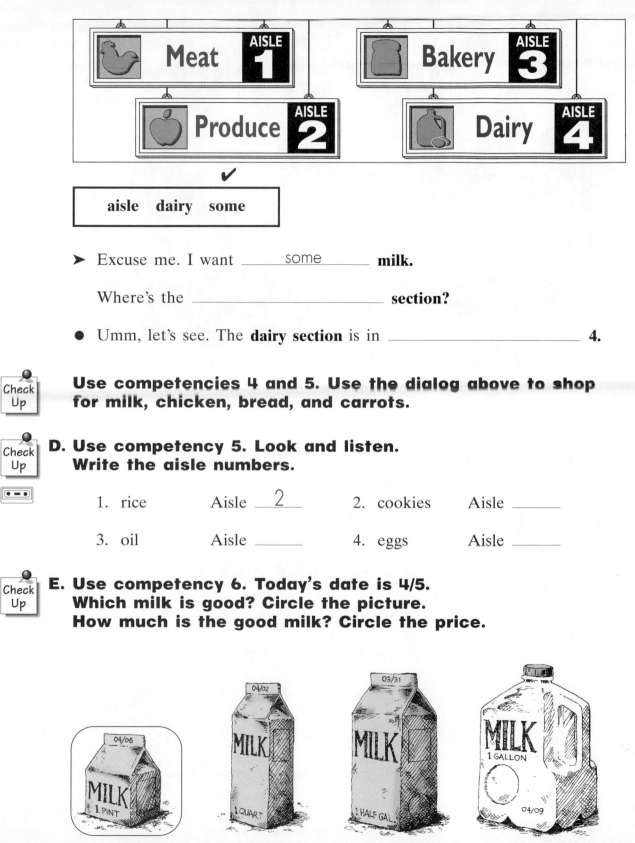

🐓	Meat	**AISLE 1**		
🍎	Produce	**AISLE 2**		
🍞	Bakery	**AISLE 3**		
🥛	Dairy	**AISLE 4**		

✔

aisle   dairy   some

➤ Excuse me. I want _____some_____ **milk.**

  Where's the _____ **section?**

● Umm, let's see. The **dairy section** is in _____ **4.**

Check Up

Use competencies 4 and 5. Use the dialog above to shop for milk, chicken, bread, and carrots.

Check Up

D. Use competency 5. Look and listen. Write the aisle numbers.

1. rice   Aisle __2__   2. cookies   Aisle _____

3. oil   Aisle _____   4. eggs   Aisle _____

Check Up

E. Use competency 6. Today's date is 4/5. Which milk is good? Circle the picture. How much is the good milk? Circle the price.

04/02   03/31   04/06   04/09

(39¢)   69¢ $1.15 $1.99

6 Shopping

Where are the people? What's happening? What do you think?

Listen and practice the chant.

What size do you wear?

    I wear a small.

Do you want a coat to wear this fall?

    No, I'd like a shirt and I prefer blue.

This shirt is cotton. It'll fit you.

    Is it on sale? It looks very nice.

It's 10% off the regular price.

    That's fine with me. Where do I pay?

Pay the cashier. Have a nice day!

Starting Out

A. Look and read.

1. Mr. Tran has a job interview.
   He wants a new suit and tie.
   Shirts are on sale.
   He's buying a new shirt, too.

2. It's winter.
   Ms. Barker wants a winter coat.
   Hats and gloves are on sale.
   She's buying a hat, too.
   She doesn't want gloves.

B. Practice the dialog.

➤ I want to buy **a new suit for work.**

● OK. What color do you want?

➤ **Brown or blue.**

● **This blue suit is** nice. I think **it's** your size.

➤ Can I try **it** on?

● Yes, of course. The dressing room is around the corner.

➤ Thank you.

C. Work with a partner.
   Use the dialog in B to shop for clothes you want to buy.

Talk It Over

A. Myra is shopping for a new jacket. Practice the dialog.

➤ Excuse me. Where are the **jackets?**

● They're over here. What size do you wear?

➤ **Medium. That blue jacket** is nice. How much **is it?**

● **$39.95.** Do you want to try **it** on?

➤ Yes, thanks.
   OK, I'll take **it.**

● Fine. How are you paying, cash or check?

➤ **Cash.**

**B. Look at the clothes.
What do you want to buy?
Circle the numbers.**

1   $19.95

2   $40.00

3   $24.95

4   $7.99

**C. Work with a partner.
Use the dialog in A to buy the clothes you circled in B.**

Word Bank

A. Study the vocabulary.

Clothes		
belt	tie	
blouse	T-shirt	
coat	underwear	
dress		
gloves	**Size**	
hat	small (S)	
jacket	medium (M)	
jeans	large (L)	
pants	extra-large (XL)	

Useful Language
How much (is it)?
Can I try (it) on?
I'll take (it).
Cash or check?
(It's) on sale.

		Colors	
shirt	dressing room	**Colors**	orange
shorts	sales clerk	black	pink
skirt		blue	purple
socks	shoes	brown	red
suit	boots	gray	white
sweater	sneakers	green	yellow

B. Work with a small group.
What are people in your group wearing?
Complete the chart. Use words from A.

Clothes	Color	Size (optional)

Listening

About You

A. Look, listen, and circle the letter of the correct tag.

1.

a. L $10.00

b. M $10.00

2.

a. M $7.99

b. M $9.99

3.

a. XL $24.00

b. L $26.00

B. What are the people buying?
Look, listen, and number the pictures in column A.

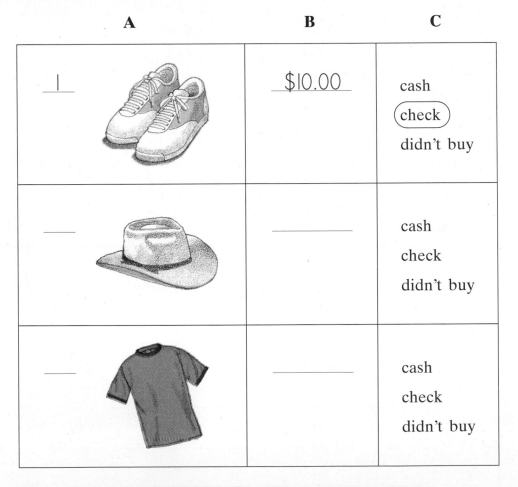

A	B	C
1	$10.00	cash / (check) / didn't buy
		cash / check / didn't buy
		cash / check / didn't buy

About You

Listen again and write the price in column B.

Listen again. Did the people buy the clothes?
How did they pay?
Circle *cash*, *check*, or *didn't buy* in column C.

Reading

A. Look and read.

| Fits sizes 8–11
$5.00 | Medium
$15.00 | Medium
$15.00 | Size 10
$19.00 |

John's buying these clothes. The clothes are on sale.

1. What's John buying?
2. How much does each item cost?

About You

**B. Read the receipt. Count John's change.
Answer the questions.**

RECEIPT

socks	$ 5.00
sweater	15.00
sweater	15.00
sneakers	<u>19.00</u>
Subtotal	54.00
Tax	2.70
Total	56.70
Amount Paid	60.00
Change	3.30

1. How much money did John give to the cashier? $60.00

2. How much change did John get?   _____

3. Did John get the right change?   _____

**C. Work with a small group.
What do you think John should do?**

Structure Base

A. Study the examples.

I want	this	shirt.
	that	

I want	these	shoes.
	those	

B. Lily's daughter, Sonia, wants new clothes for school. Sonia and Lily are shopping together. Complete the dialog. Write the correct word.

➤ Mom, I want _____this_____ (this, these) sweater.

● OK, Sonia. I'll buy _____ (that, those) sweater for you.

➤ Thanks. I want _____ (this, these) shoes and

_____ (that, those) socks.

● Well, you have money, too. You can buy

_____ (that, those) shoes and socks.

➤ OK.

C. Study the examples.

What size	do	I	wear?
		we	
		you	
		they	
	does	he	
		she	

I	wear	size 8.
We		
You		
They		
He	wears	
She		

**D. The salesclerk is helping Sonia find a jacket.
Complete the dialog. Follow the examples in C.**

■ <u>What</u> color _____ you want?

➤ I want red.

■ _____ size _____ you wear?

➤ I don't know. Mom, _____ size _____ I wear?

● You _____ a large.

E. Study the examples.

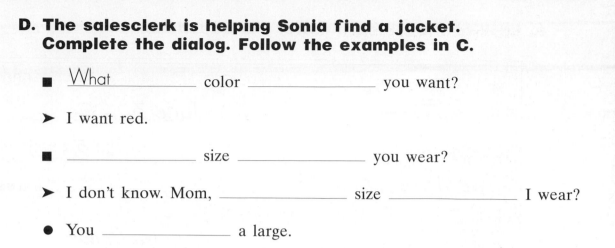

Do	I we you they	wear a small?
Does	he she	

Yes,	I	do.
	she	does.

No,	I	don't.
	she	doesn't.

**F. Sonia wants gloves, too. Lily is helping Sonia find gloves.
Complete the dialog. Follow the examples in E.**

➤ <u>Do</u> you _____ green?

● No, I _____.

➤ _____ you _____ black?

➤ Yes, I _____.

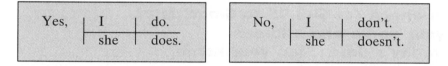

**G. Work with a partner.
You and your partner are shopping for clothes together.
Follow the examples in A, C, and E to talk about
clothes you want.**

Write It Down

A. Look at the check. Answer the questions.

```
                                                              680
    Luisa Gamboa
    601 Madison Ave.
    Albany, NY 12212
                                    June 3  19 94

PAY TO THE   Buy-Mart                           $  26.59
ORDER OF
              Twenty-six and 59/100 _____ DOLLARS

TOWN BANK
700 Hamiton St.
Albany, NY 12204
                                        Luisa Gamboa
FOR _____        _____

     ⑈111904603⑈:605 5000 ⑈
```

1. How much is the check for? _____ $26.59 _____

2. Who's writing the check? _____

3. Who's receiving the check? _____

4. What's the date of the check? _____

B. Write a check for $49.95 to Smart Mart.
Print your name and address.
Write today's date. Sign your name.

```
                                                              164
    _____
    _____
    _____        _____ 19 _____

PAY TO THE  _____          $ _____
ORDER OF
             Forty-nine and 95/100 _____ DOLLARS

LANDMARK BANK
125 Shady Lane
Shamrock, Texas 79079

FOR _____        _____

     ⑈111904603⑈:605 5000 ⑈
```

One To One

1. **Two friends want some new clothes.**
   Clothes are on sale at Buy-Mart and at Smart Shop.
   One friend has the Smart Shop ad.
   The other has the Buy-Mart ad.
   Practice the dialog.

   ➤ Are **jackets** on sale at **Smart Shop?**
   ● Yes, they are.
   ➤ How much are they?
   ● They're $40.00.

2. **Find out the prices at Smart Shop. Ask Student B.**
   Follow the dialog in I. Write the information.

   a. ____$40.00____   b. _____   c. _____

3. **Tell Student B the prices at Buy-Mart.**
   Follow the dialog in I.

4. **Switch roles. Turn to page 82. Complete 2 and 3.**

1. **Two friends want some new clothes.**
   Clothes are on sale at Buy-Mart and at Smart Shop.
   One friend has the Smart Shop ad.
   The other has the Buy Mart ad.
   Practice the dialog.

   ➤ Are **jackets** on sale at **Smart Shop?**
   ● Yes, they are.
   ➤ How much are they?
   ● They're **$40.00.**

2. **Tell Student A the prices at Smart Shop.**
   Follow the dialog in 1.

3. **Find out the prices at Buy-Mart. Ask Student A.**
   Follow the dialog in 1. Write the information.

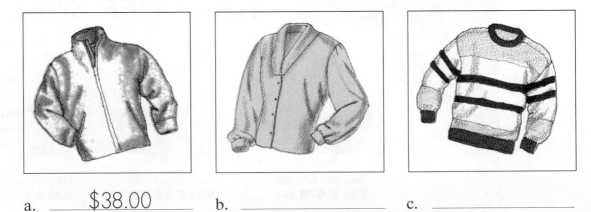

   a. ___$38.00___   b. _____   c. _____

4. **Switch roles. Turn to page 81. Complete 2 and 3.**

Extension

A. Look at the charts. Which chart has your sizes?

Neck · **Sleeve** · **Chest** · **Waist** · **Hips**

WOMEN'S SIZES									
Size	P	S	M		L		XL		
	4	6	8	10	12	14	16	18	20
Chest	33	34	35	36	38	40	42	44	46
Waist	25	26	27	28	29	31	32	34	35
Hips	35	36	38	39	40	42	43	45	46

MEN'S SIZES				
Size	S	M	L	XL
Neck	14–14 ½	15–15 ½	16–16 ½	17–17 ½
Chest	34–36	38–40	42–44	46–48
Waist	28–30	32–34	36–38	40–42
Sleeve	32–33	33–34	34–35	35–36

About You

B. Use the chart in A that has your sizes. Write your sizes.

Women

	Number Size	Letter Size
Dress	_____	_____
Blouse	_____	_____
Skirt	_____ (waist)	_____
Pants and jeans	_____ (hips)	_____

Men

	Number Size	Letter Size
Shirt	_____ (neck)	_____
	_____ (sleeve)	
Pants and jeans	_____ (waist)	
Suit coat and sport coat	_____ (chest)	_____
	_____ (sleeve)	

Unit 6

83

Can you use the competencies?

☐ 1. Identify clothes by article, size, and color
☐ 2. Shop for clothes
☐ 3. Read clothing ads and comparison shop
☐ 4. Listen for and say prices and totals
☐ 5. Read size tags, price tags, and receipts
☐ 6. Write checks

A. Review competencies I and 2. Complete the dialog.

✔

| color   much   size   take |

➤ I want **a new winter coat.**

● What _____size_____ do you wear?

➤ **Medium.**

● What _____ do you want?

➤ I want **blue.** How _____ **is that blue coat?**

● **It's $39.00.**

➤ **OK, I'll** _____ it.

Check Up

**Use competencies I and 2.
Use the dialog above to talk about
clothes you want to buy.**

Check Up

**B. Use competency 3. Look at the ads. Where would
you shop? Circle the number of the ad. Tell why.**

1.

Long's Department Store

$30.00 $40.00 $13.00

2.

ARE'S DEPARTMENT STORE

$24.00 $30.00 $10.00

BIG SAVINGS!

C. Use competency 4. Listen. Circle the prices.

pants:	($14.40)	$40.14
gloves:	$11.00	$14.00
T-shirts:	$ 6.99	$ 7.89

D. Use competency 5. John bought these things.
Read the tags. Look at John's receipt. Is it correct?

SWEATER
L
$15.99

SUIT
36
$89.00

TIE
$5.99

1 Sweater..................	$15.99
1 Suit	99.00
1 Tie	5.99
Subtotal	$120.98
Tax	6.05
Total	127.03
Amount Paid...............	130.00
Change	2.97

E. Use competency 6. Write a check for $39.40 to
Smart Shop. Print your name and address.
Write today's date. Sign your name.

640

19 _____

PAY TO THE
ORDER OF _____ $ ☐

Thirty-nine and 40/100 _____ DOLLARS

CENTRAL BANK
4230 Main St.
Pleasant City, OH 43228

FOR _____

⑈11190460⑉⑆60550001

Home

Unit Competencies

1. Identify rooms, furniture, and kinds of housing
2. Read for-rent ads
3. Ask for utilities to be turned on
4. Ask for simple repairs

What are the people doing? What are they saying? What do you think?

Listen and practice the chant.

The kitchen sink is broken.
There's water on the floor.

It's ruining the carpet.
And running out the door.

This leaking pipe is such a mess.
What are we going to do?

Let's call a plumber right away.
Let's call the owner, too!

Starting Out

A. This is Wen-tao and Ji-ling's apartment. Look and read.

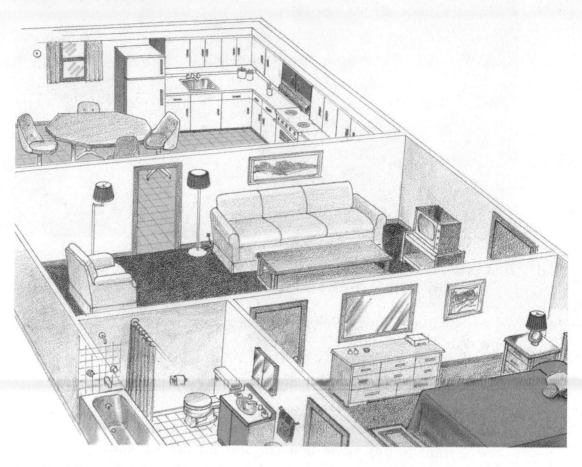

1. Wen-tao likes to cook.
   There's a stove and a
   refrigerator in the kitchen.
   There's a smoke detector, too.

2. The bedroom's large.
   There's a bed and a
   dresser in the bedroom.
   There's a rug near the bed.

3. The bathroom's small.
   There's soap on the sink.
   There are towels beside
   the sink.

4. Wen-tao and Ji-ling visit
   with friends in the living room.
   They have a nice sofa and chair
   in the living room.

Wen-tao and Ji-ling like their home.
The rent is $450 a month. The deposit is $200.

About
You

B. Answer the questions.

1. What's Wen-tao and Ji-ling's apartment like?
2. How much is the rent? Is that a lot of money?
3. What's your home like?

Talk It Over

 **A. Lisa and Cynthia are in the cafeteria.
They're talking about their homes. Practice the dialog.**

➤ I live in **a house.** What kind of home do you have?

● **An apartment.**

➤ What's it like?

● **Well, there's one bedroom and one bathroom.**

➤ Is the **bedroom large?**

● **Not really.** There's **only a bed, a dresser, and a lamp.**
  I want to **buy some new curtains for the window.**

➤ Oh. I want to **put a new sofa and a coffee table in my living room.**

 B. Write about your home.

Room	What's in the room?
Living Room	
Kitchen	
Bedroom	
Bathroom	

 **C. Work with a partner.
Use the dialog in A to talk about your home.**

Word Bank

A. Study the vocabulary.

100	one hundred
200	two hundred
300	three hundred
400	four hundred
500	five hundred
600	six hundred
700	seven hundred
800	eight hundred
900	nine hundred
1000	one thousand

Useful Language
(We) put (a sofa in our living room).
What's the matter?

apartment
house
deposit
rent

Living Room
chair
coffee table
lamp
rug
sofa
TV

Bathroom
sink
soap
toilet
towel

Kitchen
refrigerator
smoke detector
stove
table

owner
utilities

electrician
plumber

Bedroom
bed
dresser

B. Work with a partner. Use words from A to describe the furniture in the living room.

Listening

**A. Look and listen. Some people are at home.
Which rooms are they in? Write the room in column A.**

✔

bedroom	kitchen	living room

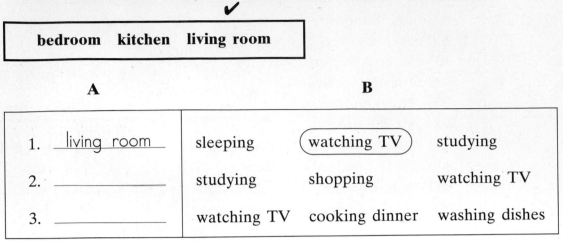

	A	**B**		
1.	living room	sleeping	(watching TV)	studying
2.	_____	studying	shopping	watching TV
3.	_____	watching TV	cooking dinner	washing dishes

**Listen again. What are the people doing?
Circle the answer in column B.**

B. Look, listen, and number the apartments.

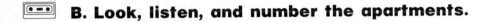

rent: _____   rent: ___$450___   rent: _____

deposit: _____   deposit: ___$100___   deposit: _____

**Listen again.
Write the rent and the deposit under the apartment.**

**C. Work with a partner. Look at the apartments in B.
Which one would you rent? Why?**

Reading

A. Newspapers have ads with apartments and houses for rent. Look and read.

Apts for Rent **Furn**	Lg 1 bdrm apt.	Apts for Rent **Unfurn**	3 bdrm, 2 ba. Lg lv rm, kit.
Sm furn 2 bdrm apt.	Parking. No pets.	1 bdrm apt, 200 Main St.	Near schools and park.
412 Albany St.	$350 mo. $200 deposit.	Very nice area.	$800 mo/$800 deposit.
$500 mo, $250 deposit.	Some utils.	$300 rent, $100 deposit.	Utils incl.
Call 555-0211 after 5.	Bay Apts, 555-9250	Sm pet OK. 555-5922	Call 555-7391

B. Read the words. Write the abbreviations. Use the ads in A.

1. apartment   _____apt_____   2. bathroom _____

3. bedroom _____   4. furnished _____

5. included _____   6. kitchen _____

7. large _____   8. living room _____

9. month _____   10. small _____

11. unfurnished _____   12. utilities _____

C. Answer the questions about the ads.

1. Is the apartment on Albany Street furnished?   _____yes_____

   How many bedrooms are there?   _____

2. Can you have pets at Bay Apartments?   _____

   Is there parking?   _____

3. How much is the rent for the apartment on Main Street?   _____

   How much is the deposit?   _____

4. How many bathrooms are there in the 3-bedroom apartment?   _____

   Are utilities included?   _____

Structure Base

A. Study the examples.

How many	bedrooms	are there?
	bathrooms	

There	are	two bedrooms.
There's		one bathroom.

B. Chris is asking Ms. Orozco about an apartment. Use the words from A.

➤ How many bedrooms _____are there_____?

● _____ two bedrooms.

➤ How many bathrooms _____?

● _____ one bathroom.

C. Study the examples.

Is	there	a deposit?
Are		rugs in the living room?

Yes, there	is.
	are.

No, there	isn't.
	aren't.

D. Chris wants to know more about the apartment. Complete the dialog. Use the words from A and C.

➤ _Are there_____ rugs in the apartment?

● _____ rugs in the bedrooms.

➤ _____ rugs in the living room?

● No, _____.

➤ The ad says the rent is **$450.** _____ a deposit?

● Yes, _____. There's a **$450 deposit, too.**

**E. Work with a partner. You have an apartment for rent.
Your partner is asking about it.
Follow the dialogs in B and D.**

F. Study the examples.

The chair is	in front of in back of near beside	the sofa.

**G. Look at the room.
Read the sentences. Write *yes* or *no*.**

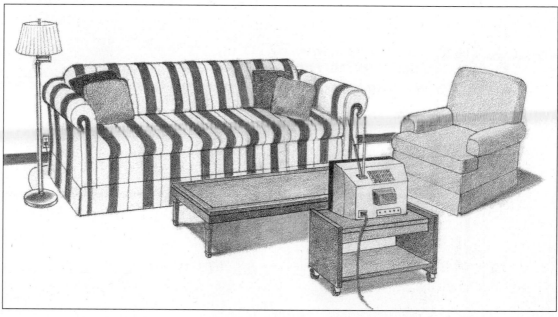

_____no_____ 1. The coffee table is in back of the chair.

_____ 2. The coffee table is in front of the sofa.

_____ 3. The lamp is near the TV.

_____ 4. The lamp is beside the sofa.

_____ 5. The chair is near the sofa.

**H. Work with a partner. Talk about a room in your home.
Where's the furniture? Follow the examples in F and G.**

Write It Down

A. Look and read. What's the matter?

The roof leaks.   The light is broken.   The toilet is
                                                       stopped up.

**B. Ms. Anaya wants repairs.
She's writing a note to the owner. Complete the note.**

✔

apartment   call   plumber   stopped   toilet

Dear Mr. Soto,

    The _____toilet_____ in my _____

is _____ up.

    Please _____ a _____

right away.

        Thank you.

        Ms. Anaya

 **C. What's the matter at your house or apartment?
Write a note on a sheet of paper. Ask for repairs.**

About
You

I. Practice the dialog.

➤ How much is the **rent** at **102 First Street?**

● It's **$500.**

➤ How many **bedrooms** are there?

● **Two.**

➤ How many **bathrooms** are there?

● **One.**

➤ Is it **furnished?**

● **No.**

2. You're calling about the apartments. Ask Student B. Follow the dialog in I. Write the information.

Address:	102 First Street	215 West Avenue
Rent:	$500	
Number of bedrooms:	2	
Number of bathrooms:		
Furnished?		

3. Student B is calling about the apartments. Tell Student B the information. Follow the dialog in I.

APARTMENTS

1 bdrm, 1 ba furn apt for rent.
210 Oak Avenue
$450 mo., $450 deposit.
Phone 555-3101.

1786 Burgess Street
2 bdrm, 1 ba apt., unfurn.
2nd floor.
$450 rent, $300 deposit.
555-2509.

4. Switch roles. Turn to page 96. Complete 2 and 3.

I. Practice the dialog.

➤ How much is the **rent** at **102 First Street?**

● It's **$500.**

➤ How many **bedrooms** are there?

● **Two.**

➤ How many **bathrooms** are there?

● **One.**

➤ Is it **furnished?**

● **No.**

2. Student A is calling about the apartments.
Tell Student A the information. Follow the dialog in I.

APARTMENTS

For Rent: 2 bdrm apt.
1 ba. Unfurn. $500 mo. rent
plus $250 deposit.
102 First Street 555-9012.

Good area! Nice apt!
Furn. 1 bdrm, 1 ba.
215 West Avenue
$425 rent, $350 deposit.
555-8453, after 5.

3. You're calling about the apartments. Ask Student A.
Follow the dialog in I. Write the information.

Address:	210 Oak Avenue	1786 Burgess Street
Rent:	$450	
Number of bedrooms:		
Number of bathrooms:		
Furnished?		

4. Switch roles. Turn to page 95. Complete 2 and 3.

Extension

 A. Practice the dialog.

> Hello. **City Gas and Electric.**
● I need the **electricity and the gas** turned on at my new **apartment.**
> What's your address?
● **545 Central Street, apartment 28.**
> And your name?
● **Eva Delgado.**
> OK. We can turn them on **tomorrow afternoon.**
● OK. Thank you.

About You **B. Work with a partner.**
You need the water turned on.
Use the dialog in A to call the City Water Company.

Can you use the competencies?

☐ 1. Identify rooms, furniture, and kinds of housing
☐ 2. Read for-rent ads
☐ 3. Ask for utilities to be turned on
☐ 4. Ask for simple repairs

A. Review competency I.
Look at the picture. Complete the sentences.

kitchen	refrigerator	table

This is the _____kitchen_____. There's a stove

and a _____ in this room.

There isn't a _____.

Check Up

Use competency I.
Use the sentences above to talk about the rooms in your home. Do you live in an apartment or a house?

B. Use competency 2.
Read the ad. Answer the questions.

1. How many bedrooms are there?   _2_

2. How many bathrooms are there?   _____

3. How much is the rent?   _____

4. How much is the deposit?   _____

> **For rent:**
> 2 bdrm, 1 ba apt, furn.
> 420 Spruce Street, Apt. J.
> Near school. Pets OK.
> $550 mo plus $200 deposit.
> Call 555-6718, evenings.

C. Review competency 3. Complete the dialog.

> turned on   water

➤ **City** _____ **Company.** May I help you?

● Yes, I need the **water** _____ at my new **house.**

➤ OK. We can do it **today.**

Use competency 3. You need the gas and electricity turned on in your home. Use the dialog above to call the City Gas and Electric company.

D. Use competency 4. Your kitchen light is broken. Complete the note to ask for repairs.

✔

> broken   electrician   light

Dear Ms. Berger,

The _____light_____ in my kitchen is _____.

Please call an _____.

Thank you.

_____ (your signature)

Health Care

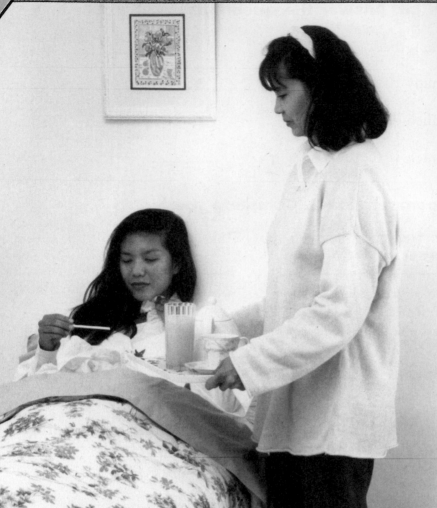

Unit Competencies

1. Identify kinds of health clinics
2. Read a thermometer
3. Make doctors' appointments
4. Talk about symptoms and injuries
5. Listen to doctors' instructions

What are the people doing? What are they saying? What do you think?

Listen and practice the chant.

> Headache. Fever.
> Sore throat, too.
> I feel awful
> With this flu.
>
> Stay in bed. Get some rest.
> I'll call Dr. Boone.
> Take vitamin C. Drink hot tea.
> And you'll feel better soon.

Starting Out

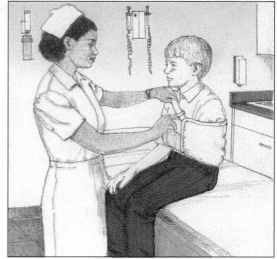

1. Ms. Garza is at City Clinic.
   She's pregnant.
   She's getting a check-up.

2. Dan is in the emergency room.
   He has a broken arm.

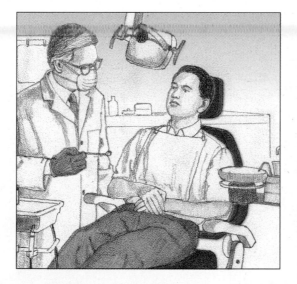

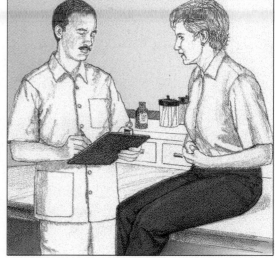

3. Mr. Li is at the dentist's office.
   He has a toothache.

4. Ms. Hill is at the doctor's office.
   She has a stomachache.

B. Answer the questions.

1. Where are the people?
2. Why are they there?
3. Where do you go when you get sick?

Talk It Over

**A. Gustavo Delgado is getting a check-up.
Practice the dialog.**

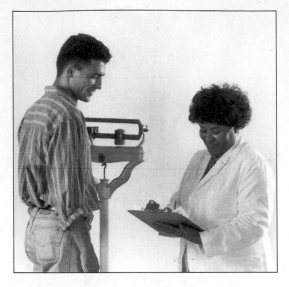

➤ Please get on the scale,
  Mr. Delgado.
  OK, you weigh 150 pounds.

➤ Now, let me look at your
  throat. Say "ah."
● Ahhh.
➤ OK. That looks good.

➤ Now breathe in.

➤ And now breathe out.
  Excellent. You're in very
  good health.

About
You

**B. Work with a partner. Look at the pictures in A.
Take turns giving the instructions.
Do what your partner says.**

Word Bank

A. Study the vocabulary.

backache   well
broken (arm)   pregnant
a cold
cough   check-up
earache   clinic
fever   dentist
the flu   doctor
headache   emergency
sore throat   hospital
stomachache   medicine
toothache   nurse
                  office

sick
tired

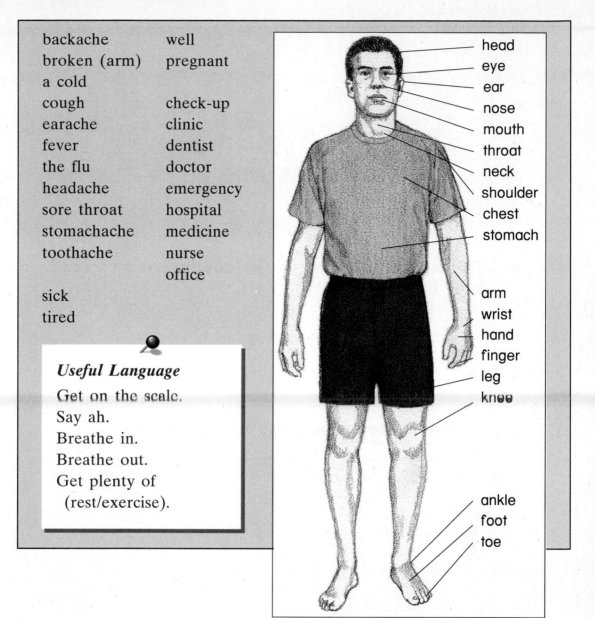

head
eye
ear
nose
mouth
throat
neck
shoulder
chest
stomach
arm
wrist
hand
finger
leg
knee
ankle
foot
toe

> 📌 *Useful Language*
> Get on the scale.
> Say ah.
> Breathe in.
> Breathe out.
> Get plenty of
>   (rest/exercise).

B. Work with a partner. You're at the doctor's office. Show where it hurts. Tell where it hurts. Use words from A.

1. You have a stomachache.
2. You have a broken wrist.
3. You have a sore throat.
4. You have a headache.

C. Work with a partner. Talk about where you go for health care. Who works there? Use words from A.

Listening

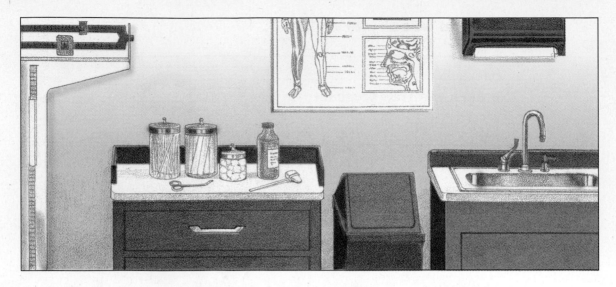

A. **Look and listen. Who do the people need to see?**
   Circle the answer.

1. (doctor)   dentist

2. doctor   dentist

3. doctor   dentist

B. **Look and listen. Complete the sentences.**

✔

| check-up   flu   stomachache |

1. David has a _____stomachache_____.

2. Ms. Long needs a _____.

3. Ms. Buzek has the _____.

About You

Listen again. What does the doctor say?
Complete the sentences.

✔

| candy   months   sleep |

1. Stop eating so much ____candy____.

2. Come back in six _____.

3. Get plenty of _____. Drink water, tea, and juice.

104   Unit 8

Reading

A. Look and read.

NEW CLINIC OFFERS LOW-COST HEALTH CARE

John Jones is sick. He wants to see a doctor. Where can he go?
Starting next week he can go to the new Community Health Clinic.
It opens on Monday, July 1, at 408 West 10th Street.

Community Health Clinic is not a hospital. But many doctors and
nurses work there to provide health care at a low cost.

Everyone can get excellent health care at the clinic.
These are some of the services:
• General check-ups
• Pregnancy check-ups
• Children's health care
• Non-emergency illnesses and injuries
• Treatment of many <u>minor</u> emergencies

The Community Health Clinic is having a special Health Fair Day
on July 1. You can meet the doctors and nurses, get a free blood
pressure check, and get shots for you and your children.
For information, call 555-8924.

B. Answer the questions. Write *yes* or *no*.

1. Is the Community Health Clinic a hospital?   no

2. Do doctors work at the clinic?   _____

3. Is the clinic expensive?   _____

4. Can you get a check-up at the clinic?   _____

5. Can you go there if you have a cold or the flu?   _____

C. Work with a small group. Answer the questions.

1. Why do people go to health clinics? Give more than one reason.
2. Do you go to health clinics? Why or why not?

Structure Base

A. Study the examples.

How	do	I we you they	feel?
	does	he she	

I We You They	feel	sick.
He She	feels	

B. Ms. Davidov and her daughter are at the doctor's office. Complete the dialog. Use the words from A.

➤ Hi, Ms. Davidov. How _____do_____ you _____?

● I _____ fine, Dr. Agoyo. But Sophia is sick.

➤ Oh, no. How _____ she _____?

● She _____ terrible. She has a stomachache.

➤ Come here, Sophia. Let's see what we can do for you.

C. Work with a small group. Talk about how you feel. Follow the examples in A.

About You

D. Study the examples.

I We You They	have	the flu.
He She	has	

E. Look at the pictures. Complete the sentences. Use the words in D.

She has _____ a **stomachache.**

_____ a **fever.**

_____ the **flu.**

_____ a **broken arm.**

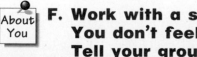

F. Work with a small group.
You don't feel well. What's the matter?
Tell your group. Follow the sentences in E.

Write It Down

A. You don't feel well.
You go to the Community Health Clinic.
Complete the form. Write about yourself.

Community Health Clinic
Patient Information Form

✚ CHC

Name _Manuel Villagrana_

Address _P.O. Box 1225_ Telephone Number _831 385 000_

Date of Birth _1/16/70_ Age _34_ Male _✓_ Female _____

Who can we call in an emergency?

Name _Antonio martines_

Telephone Number _385 8970_

What are your symptoms? Check here. (✓)

_✓_ backache   _____ headache

_____ cough   _✓_ sore throat

_____ earache   _____ stomachache

_____ fever   _____ other (Write here.) _____

Answer *yes* or *no*.

Are you pregnant? _no_

Have you ever been in the hospital? _Si_

If yes, why? _____

Do you exercise? _Si_

Do you take any medicine? _no_

If yes, what medicine? _____

Signature _manul martines_ Date _____

108

Unit 8

1. Practice the dialog.

➤ What's the matter with **Calvin**?

● **He** has a **backache**.

2. What's the matter with them? Ask Student B. Follow the dialog in I. Write the information.

a. Calvin ___has a___   b. Dee ___TooTache___   c. Mei-hua _____

___backache___ .   _____ .   _____ .

3. What's the matter with them? Tell Student B. Follow the dialog in I.

a. Albert   b. Marilyn   c. Yong-shik

4. Switch roles. Turn to page IIO. Complete 2 and 3.

5. Talk with a partner.
What should the people do?
Who should go to the dentist?
Who should go to the doctor?
Who should stay home and rest?

I. Practice the dialog.

➤ What's the matter with **Calvin?**

● **He** has a **backache.**

About You

2. What's the matter with them?
Tell Student A. Follow the dialog in I.

 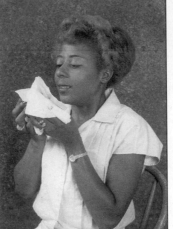 

a. Calvin   b. Dee   c. Mei-hua

About You

3. What's the matter with them? Ask Student A.
Follow the dialog in I. Write the information.

a. Albert ___has a___   b. Marilyn _____   c. Yong-shik _____

___headache___ .   _____ .   _____ .

4. Switch roles. Turn to page 109. Complete 2 and 3.

5. Talk with a partner.
What should the people do?
Who should go to the dentist?
Who should go to the doctor?
Who should stay home and rest?

Extension

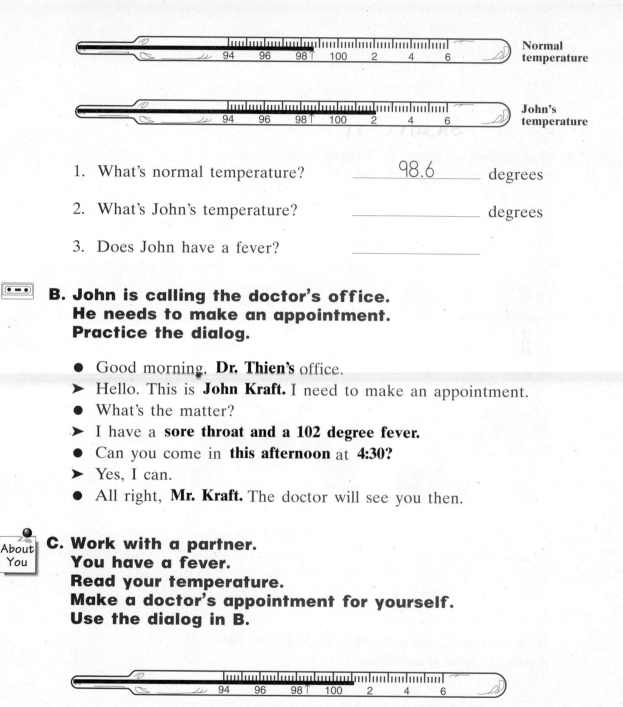

A. Study the thermometers.
Answer the questions.

Normal temperature

John's temperature

1. What's normal temperature? _____98.6_____ degrees

2. What's John's temperature? _____ degrees

3. Does John have a fever? _____

B. John is calling the doctor's office.
He needs to make an appointment.
Practice the dialog.

- ● Good morning. **Dr. Thien's** office.
- ➤ Hello. This is **John Kraft.** I need to make an appointment.
- ● What's the matter?
- ➤ I have a **sore throat and a 102 degree fever.**
- ● Can you come in **this afternoon** at **4:30?**
- ➤ Yes, I can.
- ● All right, **Mr. Kraft.** The doctor will see you then.

C. Work with a partner.
You have a fever.
Read your temperature.
Make a doctor's appointment for yourself.
Use the dialog in B.

Check Your Competency

Can you use the competencies?

☐ 1. Identify kinds of health clinics
☐ 2. Read a thermometer
☐ 3. Make doctors' appointments
☐ 4. Talk about symptoms and injuries
☐ 5. Listen to doctors' instructions

**A. Use competency I. Where are they?
Complete the sentences.**

✔

| dentist's office   doctor's office   emergency room |

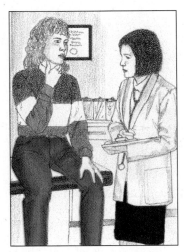 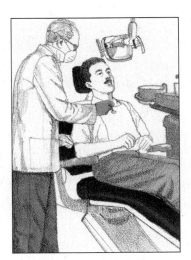 

1. Leah has a sore throat. She's at

   the doctor's office .

2. Mohamed has a toothache. He's at

   _____ .

3. Mr. Robledo has a broken arm. He's at

   _____ .

**B. Use competency 2. Read Jill's temperature.
Answer the questions.**

94 96 98↑ 100 2 4 6   **Jill's temperature**

1. What's Jill's temperature?   _____ degrees
2. Normal temperature is 98.6 degrees.
   Does Jill have a fever?   _____

C. Review competencies 3 and 4. Complete the dialog.

✔

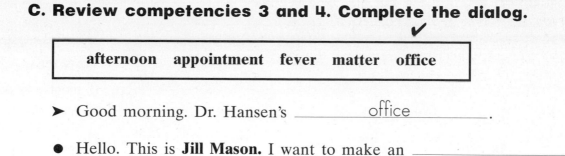

| afternoon appointment fever matter office |

➤ Good morning. Dr. Hansen's _____office_____.

● Hello. This is **Jill Mason.** I want to make an _____.

➤ What's the _____?

● **I have a** high _____.

➤ Can you come in this _____ at 4:00?

● **Yes, I can. Thanks.**

 Use competencies 3 and 4. Use the dialog above to make a doctor's appointment for yourself.

D. Use competency 5. Look and listen. What does the doctor say to do? Number the pictures from 1–5.

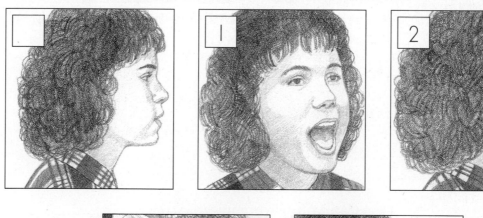

9 Employment

Where are the people? What are they saying? What do you think?

Listen and practice the chant.

I need a job.

What can you do?
Can you drive a cab?
Or fix a shoe?

I can drive a cab
And fix cars, too.

Then I can find a job for you.
Complete this application today.
And you can start work right away.

Starting Out

➤ Can you paint houses, Pedro?

● Yes, I can. I was a painter in my country.

➤ How long were you a painter?

● For 23 years.

➤ Can you cook, Mu-tan?

● Yes, I can. I was a cook in my country.

➤ How long were you a cook?

● From 1986 to 1988.

About You

B. Answer the questions.

1. What can the people do? What did they do in their countries?
2. What jobs can you do? What did you do in your country?

Talk It Over

A. Look and read.

1. cab driver

2. gardener

3. plumber

4. housekeeper

5. child care worker

6. mechanic

B. Practice the dialog.

➤ My name is Ricardo. I'm looking for a job.
● Can you drive a cab?
➤ Yes, I can.
● Do you have any experience?
➤ Yes, I was a cab driver for five years.

C. Talk to other students. Write the students' names.

About You

1. _Ricardo_ can drive a cab.

2. _____ can grow plants.

3. _____ can fix sinks.

4. _____ can clean houses and make beds.

5. _____ can take care of children.

6. _____ can paint houses.

Word Bank

A. Study the vocabulary.

Skills
bake
clean (houses)
cook
drive (a truck)
fix (sinks)
grow (plants)
make (beds)
paint (houses)
take care of
    (children)

application
apply

> *Useful Language*
> What did you do in your country?
> Do you have any experience?

company
experience
help-wanted ads
in person
interview

Jobs
child care worker
cook

(cab) driver
gardener
housekeeper
mechanic
painter
plumber

 B. Use words from A to complete the sentences.

1. A gardener _____grows_____ plants.

2. A housekeeper _____ houses.

3. A painter _____ houses and other buildings.

4. A mechanic _____ cars, buses, or trucks.

5. A child care worker _____ children.

6. A plumber _____ sinks.

7. A bus driver _____ a bus.

 C. Work with a small group. Talk about jobs. What can you do? What job do you want?

Listening

**A. Three people are interviewing for jobs.
Look and listen. What were their jobs before?
Circle the jobs in column A.**

	A Job	**B** Skill
1.	bus driver **(mechanic)** gardener	fix buses drive buses **(fix cars)**
2.	cook mechanic housekeeper	drive a bus cook bake cakes
3.	cab driver truck driver mechanic	cook in a hotel drive a truck drive a bus

**Listen again. What can they do now?
Circle the skills in column B.**

**B. Soo-ha Lee is calling about a job. Look and listen.
Read the questions. Circle the answers.**

1. What job is Soo-ha calling about?   **(gardener)**   painter
2. How long was she a gardener?   3 years   3 months
3. Can Soo-ha grow plants?   yes   no
4. Can she take care of trees?   yes   no

**C. Work with a small group.
Do you think Soo-ha will get the job?
Why or why not?**

Reading

A. Many businesses advertise jobs in newspapers. Ads for jobs are called help-wanted ads. Look and read.

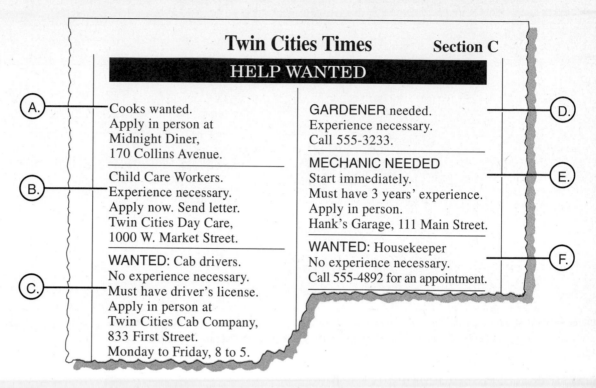

Twin Cities Times　　Section C

HELP WANTED

A. Cooks wanted.
Apply in person at
Midnight Diner,
170 Collins Avenue.

B. Child Care Workers.
Experience necessary.
Apply now. Send letter.
Twin Cities Day Care,
1000 W. Market Street.

C. WANTED: Cab drivers.
No experience necessary.
Must have driver's license.
Apply in person at
Twin Cities Cab Company,
833 First Street.
Monday to Friday, 8 to 5.

D. GARDENER needed.
Experience necessary.
Call 555-3233.

E. MECHANIC NEEDED
Start immediately.
Must have 3 years' experience.
Apply in person.
Hank's Garage, 111 Main Street.

F. WANTED: Housekeeper
No experience necessary.
Call 555-4892 for an appointment.

B. Answer the questions about the ads. Write the letters.

1. Which ads say you must apply in person?　　A, C, E

2. Which ads say to call?　　_____

3. Which ads say you need experience?　　_____

4. Which ad says to send a letter?　　_____

5. Which ad is for cab drivers?　　_____

C. Work with a partner. Talk about the ads. Would you apply for one of the jobs? Why or why not?

Structure Base

A. Study the examples.

What can	I he she we you they	do?

I He She We You They	can can't	drive a bus.

Can	I he she we you they	drive a bus?

Yes, No,	I	can. can't.

B. Use the words from A to complete the dialog.

➤ I'm looking for a job.

● What _____can_____ you do?

➤ I _____ **drive a cab.** And I _____ **fix cars.**

● _____ you **drive a bus?**

➤ No, I _____. **But I** _____ **fix buses.**

● Oh, good. I think I _____ **find a job for you.**

C. Work with a partner.
Use the dialog in B to talk about what you can do.

D. Study the examples.

I He She You	was were	a cook.

We You They	were	cooks.

E. Use the words from D to complete the sentences.

➤ What did you do in your country, Katya?

● I _was was_ a painter.

➤ How interesting. I _was_ a bus driver.

● Really? What about your brother?
Was he a bus driver, too?

➤ Yes, he _was_. We _were_ bus drivers in the same city.

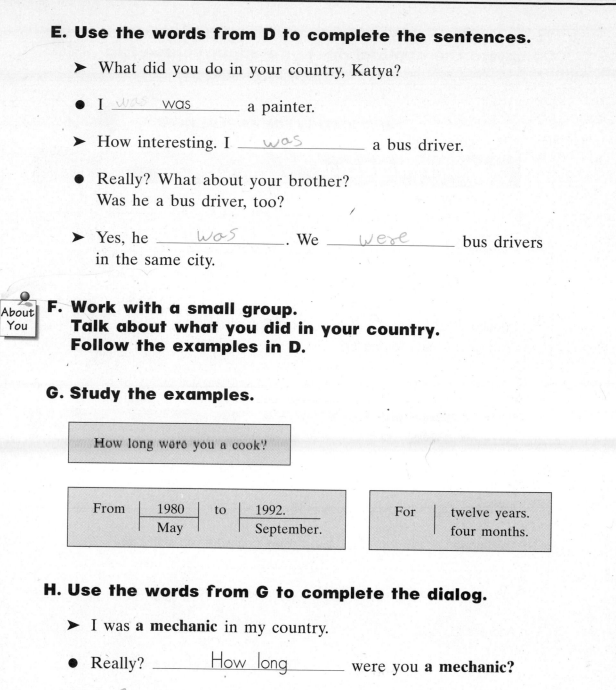

F. Work with a small group.
Talk about what you did in your country.
Follow the examples in D.

G. Study the examples.

How long were you a cook?

From	1980	to	1992.
	May		September.

For	twelve years.
	four months.

H. Use the words from G to complete the dialog.

➤ I was **a mechanic** in my country.

● Really? _How long_ were you **a mechanic?**

➤ _from_ **1976 to 1986.**

● Oh, _for_ **ten years.** That's a long time.

➤ Yes. I liked it. _How long_ were you **a gardener?**

● _for_ **two years.** _from_ **1991 to 1993.**

I. Work with a partner.
Use the dialog in H to talk about yourself.

Write It Down

A. To apply for a job, you complete a job application. Complete the application. Write about yourself.

APPLICATION FOR EMPLOYMENT

PERSONAL INFORMATION

Name _Antonio   abila_

Address _124   s. san lorenso   # 6_

_9 730_

Telephone _831 385 8090_   Social Security Number _606·70·5421_

What job are you applying for?

for   butcher chop

WORK EXPERIENCE

Job _chop_   Company _f_

Address _____

Telephone _____   How long were you at this job? _____

Job _____   Company _____

Address _____

Telephone _____   How long were you at this job? _____

READ AND SIGN

The above information is true and correct.

_____   _____
Signature   Date

122

One To One

1. Practice the dialog.

> ➤ **Antonio** needs a job.
> ● What can **he** do?
> ➤ **He** can **fix sinks.**
> ● **Acme Plumbing** needs a **plumber. He** can apply there.

**2. These people need jobs. Tell Student B.
Follow the dialog in I. Write the answers.**

Name:	a. Antonio	b. Jane	c. Dae Soo
Skills:	fix sinks	paint houses	cook and bake
Business:	Acme Plumbing		
Job:	plumber		

About You

**3. Read the ads. Follow the dialog in I.
Help Student B find jobs for people.**

HELP WANTED

BUS DRIVERS NEEDED
Must have driver's license.
Call City Bus Company,
555-8327, for appointment.

Wanted:
Child Care Workers
Apply in person.
Happy Child Center.

ANTHONY'S GARAGE
needs a mechanic.
Experience necessary.
Apply in person.
231 Market Sreet.

4. Switch roles. Turn to page 124. Complete 2 and 3.

One To One

Student B at right.

One To One   **Student B**

I. Practice the dialog.

> ➤ **Antonio** needs a job.
> ● What can **he** do?
> ➤ **He** can **fix sinks.**
> ● **Acme Plumbing** needs a **plumber. He** can apply there.

About You

2. Read the ads. Follow the dialog in I.
Help Student A find jobs for people.

HELP WANTED

Wanted: Plumber.
Apply at Acme Plumbing,
750 North Main Street,
between 8 and 12.

Kathy's Restaurant
needs a breakfast cook.
Apply in person
Monday to Friday at
3212 18th Street.

Painter wanted.
Must have experience.
Apply at Pat's Painters,
320 Jones Street.

3. These people need jobs. Tell Student A.
Follow the dialog in I. Write the answers.

Name: a. Li-hua   b. Derek   c. Henka

Skills: take care   fix cars   drive a bus
           of children

Business: _Happy Child Center_ _____ _____

Job: _____child care_____ _____ _____

_____worker_____

4. Switch roles. Turn to page I23. Complete 2 and 3.

Extension

A. These are safety warning signs. Look and read.

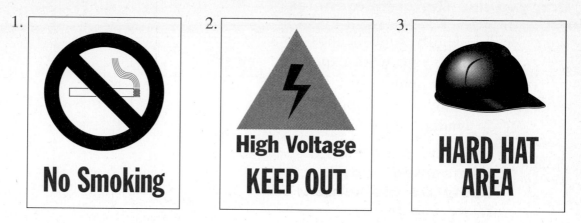

1. No Smoking

2. High Voltage KEEP OUT

3. HARD HAT AREA

 B. Look at the pictures.
   Are the people following the warnings? Write _yes_ or _no_.

1. _____yes_____ 2. _____no_____

3. _____Si_____ 4. _____no_____

Can you use the competencies?

- ☐ 1. Identify kinds of jobs
- ☐ 2. Give your work experience and skills
- ☐ 3. Read help-wanted ads
- ☐ 4. Complete job applications
- ☐ 5. Understand safety warnings

A. Use competency I.
Complete the sentences.
Write the letter.

1. A plumber __d__.

2. A painter __A__.

3. A gardener __c__.

4. A bus driver __e__.

5. A child care worker __b__.

a. paints houses

b. takes care of children

c. grows plants

✔ d. fixes sinks

e. drives a bus

B. Review competency 2. Complete the dialog.

✔

can cook do experience

➤ What can you ___do___?

● I ___con___ cook.

➤ Do you have ___experience___?

● Yes. I was a ___cook___ in my country.

Use competency 2.
Use the dialog in B to talk about yourself.

C. Use competency 3. Read the help-wanted ad. Answer the questions.

1. What's the job? _____mechanic_____

2. Do you need experience? _____Yes_____

3. Can you call to apply? _____no_____

> **MECHANIC needed.**
> Must have experience.
> Apply in person at
> 8601 Park Street.
> Monday to Friday

D. Use competency 4. Complete the job application.

APPLICATION FOR EMPLOYMENT

PERSONAL INFORMATION

Name _Antonio baskes_

Address _1245 San lorenso_

H6 Kingcity cA. 93930

Telephone _385 8090_

Social Security
Number _660 70 5423_

WORK EXPERIENCE

Job _Paints houses_

Company _wester_

Address _3! estrit_

Telephone _831 385 70 36_

How long were
you at this job? _4 Year ago_

E. Use competency 5. Look at the pictures. Are the people following the warning signs? Write yes or no.

1. _____no_____   2. _____yes_____   3. _____no_____

Transportation and Travel

Unit Competencies

1. Identify kinds of transportation
2. Read traffic signs
3. Use public transportation
4. Listen for bus numbers and fares

Where are the people? What are they talking about? What do you think?

Listen and practice the chant.

Catch a bus or ride a train.
Buy your ticket today.
Drive a car or take a plane.
Now you're on your way.

Ask for schedules, ask for fares.
Make a reservation.
You can travel near or far,
All across the nation.

Starting Out

➤ How do you get to work?
● We always take the bus.
   The fare's $1.50.

➤ How do you get to work?
● I'm in a car pool.
   We take turns driving.

➤ How does he get to work?
● He usually takes the subway.
   A token is $1.75.

➤ How do they get to work?
● They always walk.
   They never drive.

B. Answer the questions.

1. Where are the people going? How do they get there?
2. How do you get to school? How do you get to work?

Talk It Over

 A. Practice the dialogs.

➤ Excuse me.
Which bus goes to **Elm Street?**

● Bus **25.**

➤ Thanks.

➤ Excuse me.
Does this bus go to **Elm Street?**

● **Yes, it does.**

**B. Work with a partner. Where do you want to go?
Use the dialogs in A to find the bus you need.**

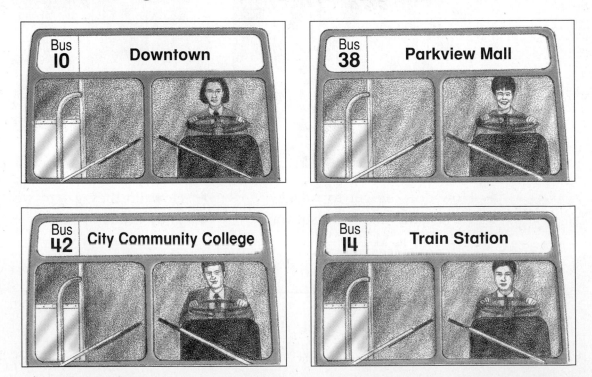

Bus **10** — Downtown

Bus **38** — Parkview Mall

Bus **42** — City Community College

Bus **14** — Train Station

Word Bank

A. Study the vocabulary.

bicycle	fare	**Traffic Signs and Signals**	
bus	station	bus stop	one way
car	token	do not enter	speed limit
subway		don't walk	stop
train		hospital	walk
car pool		no parking	yield
driver's license		no U-turn	

The red light means stop.
The yellow light means drive
with caution or slow down.
The green light means go.

B. What are they? Write the words from A.

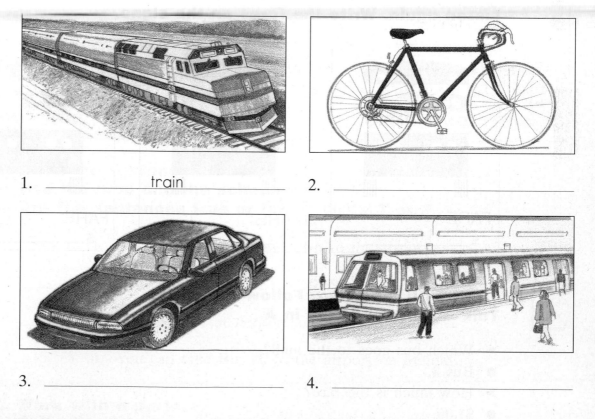

1. _____ train _____   2. _____

3. _____   4. _____

C. Work with a small group.
Talk about how you get to the supermarket and to school.

Structure Base

A. Study the examples.

always	100%
usually	↑
sometimes	↓
never	0%

I always go to the park on Sunday.

B. Work with a partner.
Use the words in A to talk about what you do.

C. Study the examples.

I always go to the bank on Friday.

I'm going to the bank right now.

D. Complete the sentences.
Write the correct form of the word.
Follow the examples in C.

1. I usually _____take_____ **(take)** the bus to school.

2. Right now I'm _____ **(wait)** for the bus.

3. Sometimes my sister _____ **(drive)** to school.

4. I never _____ **(walk)** to school.

5. I always _____ **(arrive)** at school on time.

E. Study the example.

> Which bus do I take?

F. Read the bus signs.
Write the questions.
Follow the example in E.

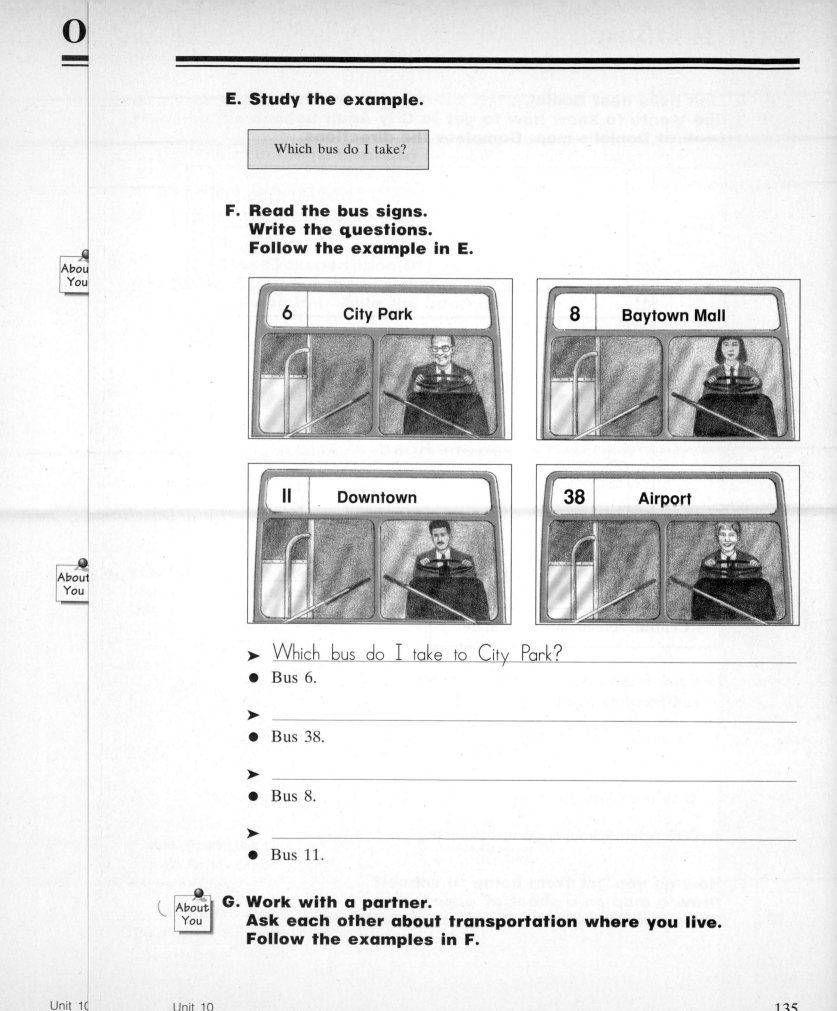

6	City Park
8	Baytown Mall
II	Downtown
38	Airport

➤ <u>Which bus do I take to City Park?</u>

● Bus 6.

➤ _____

● Bus 38.

➤ _____

● Bus 8.

➤ _____

● Bus 11.

G. Work with a partner.
Ask each other about transportation where you live.
Follow the examples in F.

I. **A customer is at City Transportation Office.**
Practice the dialog.

> ➤ I want to go to **Central Elementary School.** Which bus do I take?
> ● **32.**
> ➤ Where do I catch the bus?
> ● At **Market Street and Front Street.**

2. You're at City Transportation Office.
Student A wants to know about bus routes.
Use the bus route map. Follow the dialog in I.

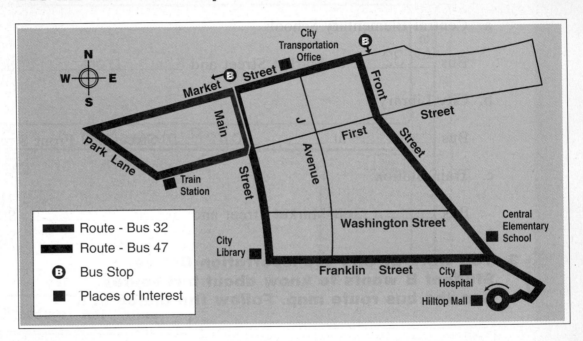

3. You're at City Transportation Office.
Ask Student A about the bus routes to these places.
Follow the dialog in I. Write the information.

a. Washington High School:

Bus ____56____ at Market Street and __J__ Avenue

b. City Park:

Bus _____ at _____ Street and Front Street

c. Post Office:

Bus _____ at _____ Street and Front Street

Extension

A. Look at the traffic signs.

B. Match the sentence with the correct sign. Write the letter.

b   1. You can't enter this street.

_____   2. This is where you catch the bus.

_____   3. You can't drive faster than 25 miles per hour.

_____   4. You can't park your car here.

_____   5. Cars can go in one direction only on this street.

_____   6. Don't cross the street now.

_____   7. There's a hospital near here.

_____   8. You have to stop completely here.

_____   9. You can't turn around here.

Can you use the competencies?

☐ 1. Identify kinds of transportation
☐ 2. Read traffic signs
☐ 3. Use public transportation
☐ 4. Listen for bus numbers and fares

Check Up

A. Use competency I. Complete the sentences.

✔

| bus   subway   car pool   walk |

1. They take the <u>subway</u> to work. 2. They take the _____ to school.

3. They're in a _____. 4. They _____ to work.

B. Use competency 2. Talk about the traffic signs.
What do you do? What don't you do?

C. Review competency 3.
Sandra is asking for directions.
Read the bus sign. Complete the dialog.

CITY BUS LINES	
BUS 5	AIRPORT
BUS 18	CITY LIBRARY
BUS 27	MIDTOWN MALL

➤ I want to go to **City Library.** Which _____bus_____ do I take?

● Take bus _____.

Use competency 3. Look at the bus sign.
You're at the City Transportation Office.
Where do you want to go?
Use the dialog above to ask about bus routes.

D. Use competency 4. Write the bus numbers in column A.

	A	B
1.		
2.		
3.		

Listen again. Write the fares in column B.

Listening Transcript

Unit 1

Listening (Page 6)
Exercise A.
Look, listen, and complete the name.

1. A: What's your first name?
    B: Mei.
    A: How do you spell that?
    B: M-E-I.
    A: Is that M-E-I?
    B: Yes. That's right.
2. A: Ana, what's your last name?
    B: Smith. S-M-I-T-H.
    A: Could you repeat that?
    B: S-M-I-T-H. Smith.
    A: Thanks, Ana.
3. A: Hi. I'm Carlos.
    B: What?
    A: Carlos. C-A-R-L-O-S.
    B: What?
    A: C-A-R-L-O-S.
    B: Oh, Carlos. Good to meet you.
4. A: What's your name?
    B: Pablo.
    A: Could you spell that, please?
    B: Sure. P-A-B-L-O.
    A: Is that P-A-B-L-O?
    B: Yes, it is.
    A: Thanks.

Exercise B.
Look, listen, and write the area code.

1. A: Sabrina, I need you to look up some area codes for me.
    B: OK, Tim. What cities?
    A: Chicago.
    B: Chicago is 312.
    A: What did you say?
    B: 312.
2. A: OK. New York City.
    B: That's 212.
    A: Right. 212. I should know that. That's my mother's area code.
3. A: Now Miami.
    B: 305.
    A: Is that 305?
    B: Yes.
4. A: OK. Washington, D.C.
    B: 202. Did you get that?

A: Yeah. 202. Thanks.
B: Is that all?
A: Yes. Thanks for your help.

Exercise C.
Look, listen, and write the number.

1. A: So your city and state are Chicago, Illinois. What's your ZIP Code?
    B: 60657.
    A: Is that 60657?
    B: Yes. It is.
2. A: Your area code?
    B: 312.
3. A: And your phone number?
    B: 555-0857.
    A: So that's 555-0857?
    B: Yes.
4. A: Do you have a Social Security number?
    B: Yes. It's 345-54-9822.
    A: Could you repeat that?
    B: Yes. It's 345-54-9822.
    A: Thanks, Mr. Rizzo. Here's your identification card.
    B: Thanks a lot.

Exercise D.
Look, listen, and complete the form.

A: Your name, please.
B: Elena Martinka.
A: How do you spell that?
B: My first name is Elena. E-L-E-N-A. My last name is Martinka. M-A-R-T-I-N-K-A.
A: That's E-L-E-N-A M-A-R-T-I-N-K-A?
B: Right.
A: Your address, Ms. Martinka?
B: 3440 Lake Street.
A: 3440 L-A-K-E S-T-R-E-E-T?
B: That's right.
A: What's your apartment number?
B: 202.
A: 202. Your city and state?
B: Miami, Florida.
A: M-I-A-M-I F-L-O-R-I-D-A. The ZIP Code?
B: 33153.
A: 33153. Your phone number, area code first.
B: (305) 555-1987.
A: That's (305) 555-1987?
B: Yes.

A: What language do you speak?
B: Russian.
A: And your Social Security number?
B: 281-39-1011.
A: 281-39-1011. Thanks, Ms. Martinka. Welcome to English class.
B: Thanks.

Unit 2

Listening (Page 20)
Exercise A.
Look, listen, and write the places on the map.

1. A: Excuse me. Where's the post office?
   B: It's next to the police station.
   A: Where?
   B: Next to the police station. The post office is on the corner of Main Street and Second Avenue.
   A: On the corner of Main Street and Second Avenue. OK. Thanks.

2. A: Excuse me. Where's the bank?
   B: Across from the supermarket.
   A: Where?
   B: Across from the supermarket, on First Avenue.
   A: Oh, on First Avenue. Is it across from the drug store, too?
   B: Yes. The bank is on the corner of First Avenue and State Street, across from the supermarket and the drug store.
   A: OK. Thanks.

3. A: I'm going to the store.
   B: What store?
   A: The store on Second Avenue.
   B: Next to the laundromat?
   A: Yes. It's between the laundromat and the fire department.
   B: Oh, yes. The store across from the park, right?
   A: Right. Do you want anything?
   B: No, thanks.

4. A: How far is the hospital from here?
   B: One block. It's on Main Street.
   A: On Main Street? Where?
   B: The hospital is on the right, across from the fire department.
   A: On the right, across from the fire

department. Thank you!

Exercise B.
Look, listen, and follow the directions. Draw a line on the map.

A: Excuse me. Where's the movie theater?
B: It's not very far. Walk north on First Avenue. Go one block.
A: Walk one block north?
B: Yes. Then, turn right on State Street. Go one block east to Second Avenue.
A: One block east to Second Avenue. OK.
B: The movie theater is on the corner, across from the supermarket.
A: OK. Thank you.

Check Your Competency (Page 29)
Exercise C.
Use competency 4. Listen to the directions. Draw a line on the map on page 28.

A: Excuse me. Where's the drug store?
B: It's on the corner of Green Street and Oak Street.
A: Where?
B: It's on the corner of Green Street and Oak Street.
A: How do I get there?
B: Go east on Main Street one block.
A: I go east on Main Street one block.
B: Yes. Turn right on Oak Street. Go one block south. The drug store is on the corner of Green Street and Oak Street. It's on the left across the street from the hospital.
A: I turn right on Oak Street and go one block south. It's on the corner of Green Street and Oak Street.
B: That's right. It's on the left across the street from the hospital.
A: On the left across the street from the hospital. Thanks.

Unit 3

Listening (Page 34)
Exercise A.
Look, listen, and write the room numbers.

1. A: Hi. I'm in Level 1 English. Where's my class?

B: Level 1 English is in room 11.
A: Room 11?
B: Yes. Room 11.
A: OK, thanks.
B: You're welcome.
2. A: Excuse me. My name is Lydia Santana. Who's my teacher?
B: What class are you in?
A: I'm in Level 2 English, room 15.
B: Room 15?
A: Yes. 15.
B: Then Mr. Bondar is your teacher.
A: Mr. Bondar?
B: Yes.
A: Thanks for helping me.
B: You're welcome.
3. A: Excuse me. Can you tell me where the Level 3 English class is?
B: It's in room 20.
A: Room 20?
B: Yes. Room 20. Ms. Franklin is your teacher.
A: Ms. Franklin is my teacher?
B: Yes, she is.
A: Thanks. She's a great teacher!
B: You're welcome.
4. A: Excuse me. What's my room number?
B: What class are you in?
A: I'm in Level 4 English.
B: Room 27.
A: Room 27?
B: Yes. Room 27.
A: OK. Thanks for helping me.
B: You're welcome.

Exercise B.
Look, listen, and write the room numbers on the map.
1. A: Where's the director's office?
B: Room 16.
A: Room 16?
B: Yes. Go left here. Then go around the corner and down the hall. Room 16 is on the left.
A: OK. Room 16, on the left. Thanks.
2. A: Excuse me. How do I get to the counselors' office?
B: Turn right. Then go left down the hall. It's next to the computer room.
A: Oh. Is it room 19?

B: Yes. The counselors' office is room 19.
A: Room 19. OK. Thanks.
3. A: Hi, Albert. Where are you going?
B: To the cafeteria.
A: Where's the cafeteria?
B: Next to the exit.
A: What room is it in?
B: The cafeteria's in room 17.

Exercise C.
Look, listen, and follow the directions.
Draw a line on the map.
A: Excuse me. Where's the library?
B: Go left here. Go around the corner and down the hall. Then turn right. The library is on the left.
A: Where?
B: Turn left and then go around the corner and down the hall. Turn right. Then the library is on the left.
A: Turn left. Go around the corner and down the hall. Turn right and it's on my left?
B: Yes. That's where the library is.
A: OK. Thanks.

Check Your Competency (Page 42)
Exercise A.
Use competency 1. Listen. Write the room numbers on the building directory.
1. A: Hi. Can you tell me where the counselors' office is?
B: It's in room 117, I think.
A: Room 117?
B: Right.
A: OK. Thanks.
B: You're welcome.
2. A: Excuse me. What room is the Level 1 English class in?
B: That's room 112.
A: Room 112?
B: Yes, 112. Do you know how to find it?
A: Yes. Thank you.
B: You're welcome.
3. A: Do you know where the library is?
B: The library? It's in room 119.
A: Library...room 119. Thanks.
B: You're welcome.
4. A: Hi. Where can I find the secretary?
B: The secretary's office is room 116.

144

A: Is that 116?
B: Right, 116.
A: OK. Thanks a lot.
B: You're welcome.

Unit 4

Listening (Page 48)
Exercise A.
Look, listen, and write the time.
1. A: I'm so sleepy this morning. What time is it?
   B: Um. Let me look. It's 9:00.
   A: 9:00! Oh no! I'm late! I have to meet my sister. Bye!
   B: See you later.
2. A: Hey, Joel, what time is your break?
   B: It's 10:45.
   A: Excuse me? 10:45?
   B: Yes.
3. A: When's your lunch break?
   B: 12:15. Would you like to go to lunch today?
   A: Yes. I'll meet you at 12:15, OK?
   B: OK. See you then.
4. A: I go home at 5:30 today.
   B: 5:30?
   A: Yes, 5:30. Can you pick me up?
   B: OK. Where?
   A: I'll be near the stairs.
   B: OK. See you then.

Exercise B.
Look, listen, and circle the date.
1. A: Excuse me. What's today's date?
   B: Monday, June 7.
   A: Excuse me?
   B: Monday, June 7.
   A: Thanks.
2. A: What day do you start school, Lily?
   B: Wednesday.
   A: What's the date Wednesday?
   B: October 26.
   A: Excuse me? Is that October 26?
   B: Yes, the twenty-sixth.
3. A: When's your birthday, Carlos?
   B: It's April 19.
   A: Excuse me? April 19?

B: Yes, April 19.
A: Hey, that's my birthday, too!

Exercise C.
Look and listen to the weather forecast. Write the number of the forecast on the line.
1. Good morning. This is the morning news. It's Saturday, the 4th of July. From New York to California, everyone is celebrating Independence Day. They are swimming, fishing, and going to the beach. The weather forecast: hot and sunny all day today.

2. Welcome to the Weather Break. It's Monday, April 7th. Today's weather will be cool and rainy. The rain and cool weather are expected to continue for the next two or three days.

Check Your Competency (Page 57)
Exercise D.
Use competencies 4 and 5. Listen to the radio weather report. Circle the time, the date, and the weather.

Good morning, everyone. You're listening to Radio WRLE, everyone's favorite radio station. The time is 8:30 on June 14. It's a beautiful Saturday morning. Here's the weather: It's warm and sunny. It will stay warm and sunny all day. It's a beautiful day to go to the park. And now here's the 8:30 news for Saturday, June 14.

Unit 5

Listening (Page 62)
Exercise A.
What are the people looking for? Look, listen, and circle the letter in column A.
1. A: Excuse me. Where can I find the rice?
   B: Let's see. Rice is on aisle 3.
   A: Aisle 3?
   B: Right.
   A: Thanks.
2. A: Excuse me.
   B: Yes. Can I help you?
   A: Yes, thanks. I'm looking for a bottle of cooking oil.

B: Cooking oil? That's on aisle 5.
A: Where?
B: Aisle 5.
A: Thank you.
B: You're welcome.
3. A: Where are the carrots?
B: Excuse me?
A: The carrots?
B: Umm, they're in the fruit and vegetable section, aisle 2.
A: Aisle 2?
B: That's right.
A: Thanks.

Listen again and write the aisle number in column B. [*Play the tape or read the transcript of Exercise A aloud again.*]

Exercise B.
Look, listen, and circle the food the people want to buy.
A: Don't forget. Lee and Bo are coming to dinner tonight.
B: That's right. What should we cook?
A: What about hamburgers and French fries? That's my favorite. Bo's too, I think.
B: Good idea. We probably need to make a shopping list.
A: OK. We need two pounds of ground beef.
B: Two pounds?
A: Yes. And we also need some potatoes.
B: How many?
A: Five should be enough.
B: What else?
A: Lettuce and tomatoes.
B: Lettuce and tomatoes.
A: OK. Here's the list: two pounds of ground beef, five potatoes, lettuce, and tomatoes. Is that right?
B: What about a cake?
A: Great idea!

Exercise C.
Listen. Look at the food you circled in B. Check off the groceries they bought. Then answer the questions.
A: Let's unpack these groceries, Francisco.
B: OK. Did we get everything?
A: Let's check the shopping list.
B: We have two pounds of ground beef?
A: Yes. Two pounds of ground beef and five potatoes.
B: Five potatoes and the lettuce and tomatoes...
A: Hey, what's this candy doing in here?
B: Candy, great! I'm hungry!
A: Wait a minute. Candy wasn't on the list. Why did you get it?
B: I just wanted some.... Oh, no, guess what! We forgot something!
A: Well, Francisco, you forgot the cake, so you'll just have to go back to the store and get one! And get some apples and oranges, too.

Check Your Competency (Page 71)
Exercise D.
Use competency 5. Look and listen. Write the aisle numbers.
1. A: Excuse me. I need some rice. Where can I find that?
B: Rice's on aisle 2.
A: Where?
B: Aisle 2.
A: All right. Thank you.
2. A: Excuse me. Where are the cookies?
B: Let's see. That'd be aisle 6.
A: Excuse me?
B: Cookies are on aisle 6.
A: Aisle 6. Thanks.
3. A: Where can I find the cooking oil?
B: Cooking oil would be on aisle 3.
A: Aisle 3. OK, thanks.
B: You're welcome.
4. A: Where can I find eggs?
B: Aisle 1.
A: Aisle 1. Good. Thank you.
B: OK. Happy shopping!

Unit 6

Listening (Page 76)
Exercise A.
Look, listen, and circle the letter of the correct tag.

1. A: Excuse me. I need some help.
   B: Yes. How can I help you?
   A: I'm interested in that blouse.
   B: The blue one?
   A: Yes, that one. How much is it?
   B: $10.00.
   A: $10.00...OK. Is there a medium?
   B: Yes. Here's a medium.
   A: May I try it on?
   B: Of course. The dressing room is over there.

2. A: Can I help you?
   B: Yes. I want some white socks.
   A: How many pairs do you want?
   B: I want several pairs of white socks.
   A: We have these packages of six pairs.
   B: I like those. How much are they?
   A: A package of six pairs is $9.99.
   B: How much?
   A: $9.99.
   B: What a bargain! I'll take one package.

3. A: Excuse me. I'm looking for a sweater.
   B: What size do you wear?
   A: Well, I'm very tall and hard to fit.
   B: You probably take an extra-large, then.
   A: How much is an extra-large?
   B: This extra-large sweater's only $24.00.
   A: How much?
   B: $24.00.
   A: I need to try it on first. Where's the dressing room?
   B: The dressing room is around the corner, on your right.
   A: Thanks.

Exercise B.
What are the people buying? Look, listen, and number the pictures in column A.

1. A: Oh, look at those sneakers. I want those for summer.
   B: They *are* cute. How much are they?
   A: $10.00.

B: $10.00? That's not bad. But that other pair is only $8.00.
A: Yes. But I like these sneakers. They're my size, too. I think I'll spend the $10.00.
B: Well, here's a cashier.
C: Hi. Will that be all?
A: Yes.
C: How are you paying?
A: By check.

2. A: Did you say you wanted a T-shirt?
   B: Yes, I did.
   A: The T-shirts on this rack are on sale.
   B: How much are they?
   A: $5.00.
   B: How much?
   A: Only $5.00.
   B: Hey, great. I'd like that blue one.
   A: OK. Do you want to try it on?
   B: No, I know I wear a large. I'll take it.
   A: Fine. How are you paying?
   B: Cash.

3. A: Excuse me. I'm looking for a hat. Are those on sale?
   B: No, they're regular price.
   A: Well, how much is that one?
   B: That hat's on sale. It's half off.
   A: How much is it now?
   B: $15.00.
   A: $15.00?
   B: Yes. Do you want that one?
   A: No, thank you. I'll keep looking.

Listen again and write the price in column B. *[Play the tape or read the transcript of Exercise B aloud again.]*

Listen again. Did the people buy the clothes? How did they pay? Circle *cash*, *check*, or *didn't buy* in column C. *[Play the tape or read the transcript of Exercise B aloud again.]*

Check Your Competency (Page 85)
Exercise C.
Use competency 4. Listen. Circle the prices.

A: How much are these clothes?
B: The pants are $14.40.
A: How much?

B: $14.40.
A: And the gloves?
B: The gloves are $11.00.
A: What about those T-shirts?
B: Those are $6.99.
A: That's $14.40 and $11.00 and $6.99.
B: The total is $34.98, including tax.
A: I'll write you a check. Did you say $34.98?
B: Yes.

Unit 7

Listening (Page 90)
Exercise A.
Look and listen. Some people are at home. Which rooms are they in? Write the room in column A.

1. A: Hi, Patty. What are you doing?
   B: Hi, Alona. I'm just sitting in the living room, watching TV.
   A: Oh. Should I call back later?
   B: No, I can talk now. In fact, would you like to come over? We can watch TV together.
   A: OK. I'll bring the popcorn and be in your living room in ten minutes!
2. A: Kathleen, where are you?
   B: I'm in the bedroom.
   A: What are you doing?
   B: Studying.
   A: Oh, OK. Let me know when you're finished, and we'll go shopping.
   B: OK. How about in a half-hour?
3. A: Ken, where are you?
   B: I'm in the kitchen, cooking dinner.
   A: Great! What are you cooking?
   B: Hamburgers.
   A: Oh, that sounds good!

Listen again. What are the people doing? Circle the answer in column B. [Play the tape or read the transcript of Exercise A aloud again.]

Exercise B.
Look, listen, and number the apartments.

1. A: Excuse me. I'm looking for a one-bedroom apartment. Do you have any available?

B: Yes, we do. We have a very nice one-bedroom near the park. It has a living room, a kitchen, and one bathroom. Are you interested?
A: Maybe. How much is the rent?
B: $450 a month.
A: $450, OK. Is there a deposit?
B: Yes. We require a $100 deposit.
A: $100 isn't bad for a deposit. When can I see it?
B: We can go over there right now.

2. A: World Realty. May I help you?
   B: Yes. I'm interested in the three-bedroom apartment you advertised. Could you tell me how many bathrooms it has?
   A: Let's see.... The three-bedroom apartment has two bathrooms. Is that what you're looking for?
   B: It sure is. We need three bedrooms and two bathrooms. The ad says the rent is $750 a month.
   A: Right. It's $750. There's also a $750 deposit.
   B: Another $750 for deposit? Wow, that's a lot!
   A: Well, it's a very nice place. Are you still interested?
   B: Yes, I guess so. I'll come down to your office later today.
   A: That'd be fine. Thanks.

3. A: Hello. I just saw the for-rent sign out front. Can you give me some information on the apartment?
   B: Sure. It's occupied right now, but I can tell you about it.
   A: That'd be fine.
   B: It has two bedrooms and one bathroom. It's got a living room, and an adjoining kitchen.
   A: Sounds good. Is it furnished?
   B: No, it's not.
   A: Well, that's fine. I'm not looking for a furnished place. I have my own furniture. How much is the rent?
   B: It's $575, and there's a $300 deposit.
   A: $575 rent, with a $300 deposit. Well, I'll think about it. Thanks for your time.
   B: You're welcome.

Listen again. Write the rent and the deposit under the apartment. *[Play the tape or read the transcript of Exercise B aloud again.]*

Unit 8

Listening (Page 104)

Exercise A.

Look and listen. Who do the people need to see? Circle the answer.

1. A: Good morning. Dr. Jacob's office.
   B: Hello. I need to make an appointment for my son to see the doctor for a check-up.
   A: OK. Your name and your son's name please?
   B: My name is Jack Woods. My son is David Woods.
   A: All right, Mr. Woods. We have an opening on Wednesday, March 28, at 4:00.
   B: March 28 at 4:00. That's fine.
   A: Good. We'll see you then.
   B: Thank you.

2. A: Good afternoon. Colton Dental Clinic.
   B: Hello. This is Jennifer Long. I need to see the dentist for a check-up.
   A: Well, the dentist can see you on June 2, at 9:15 in the morning. Is that OK?
   B: Did you say June 2?
   A: Yes, June 2.
   B: OK. And what time did you say?
   A: 9:15 in the morning. Can you be here then?
   B: Yes, that's fine.

3. A: Hello. Office of Doctors Brenner, Chen, and Brown.
   B: Hello. This is Bela Buzek. I need to make an appointment with Dr. Brown.
   A: OK. Dr. Brown can see you this Thursday at 3:30. How's that?
   B: Thursday...wait. What's the date that day?
   A: December 13. Is that all right?
   B: Oh, yes. December 13 is fine. Did you say 3:30?
   A: Yes, 3:30 in the afternoon. Please hold a moment, and I'll be back to get some more information.

Exercise B.

Look and listen. Complete the sentences.

1. A: Hello, Mr. Woods. Hi, David.
   B: Hi, Dr. Jacobs.
   C: Hi.
   A: I see you're here for a check-up, David. How do you feel today?
   C: I feel OK.
   B: He feels fine now, but he gets a lot of stomachaches.
   A: Stomachaches? How much candy do you eat?
   C: Well, I always have a candy bar at lunch. And sometimes I have another one after school.
   A: Well, David, I think you need to stop eating so much candy.
   C: Stop eating candy?
   A: That's right. You can have candy once in a while, but you can't eat it all the time. That's why you get stomachaches.
   C: Well, OK.
   B: Don't worry, Dr. Jacobs. I'll make sure he doesn't eat so much candy.

2. A: Hello, Ms. Long. I'm Dr. Kim. You're here for a check-up?
   B: Hello, Dr. Kim. Yes, just a check-up.
   A: OK. No toothaches or other problems lately?
   B: No, none at all.
   A: Well, that's good. OK, open wide.
   B: OK.
   A: OK, Ms. Long, all done. Everything seems fine.
   B: Thank you, Dr. Kim.
   A: Now, I want you to come back in 6 months for another check-up, OK?
   B: OK, thank you. See you in 6 months.

3. A: Hello, Ms. Buzek. It's good to see you again.
   B: Hello, Dr. Brown.
   A: How do you feel?
   B: Well, I feel sick. First I feel hot. Then I feel cold. I feel tired a lot, too. It started a week ago.
   A: It sounds like you have the flu.
   B: The flu? Is that serious?
   A: Not at all. It's very common this time of year.
   B: What should I do?

A: Well, generally the flu has to run its course. But you need to get plenty of sleep and drink water, tea, and juice. You should feel better in another week.

B: Water, tea, and juice?

A: Yes, and lots of sleep.

Listen again. What does the doctor say? Complete the sentences. *[Play the tape or read the transcript of Exercise B aloud again.]*

Check Your Competency (Page 113)
Exercise D.
Use competency 5. Look and listen. What does the doctor say to do? Number the pictures from 1 to 5.

A: Hello, Ms. Mason. I'm Dr. Hansen. How do you feel?

B: Not very well. I feel hot.

A: Yes. I see you have a fever. Any other symptoms?

B: Yes. My head hurts. I have a sore throat, too.

A: I think you have the flu, Ms. Mason. But I'd better give you a check-up to make sure it's the flu and not something else.

B: OK.

A: First, let's take a look at your throat. Say "ah."

B: Ahhh . . .

A: Yes. I see that it must be sore. OK, now I want to listen to your breathing. Please breathe in. OK. Now breathe out.

B: OK. How's that?

A: Well, that doesn't sound too bad. I'm sure it's the flu, though.

B: What can I do for it?

A: You need to drink water, tea, and juice.

B: What?

A: Drink water, tea, and juice. Also, get plenty of sleep.

B: OK. Drinking water, tea, and juice and sleeping. Is that all?

A: Yes. You should feel better in a few days.

B: Thank you, Doctor.

Unit 9

Listening (Page 118)
Exercise A.
Three people are interviewing for jobs. Look and listen. What were their jobs before? Circle the jobs in column A.

1. A: Hello. My name is Sue Weston. Welcome to the job fair.

    B: Hello. I'm Pedro Mendoza. It's nice to meet you. I'm here to look for a job.

    A: What kind of work are you looking for, Mr. Mendoza?

    B: I'm a mechanic. I've been a mechanic for six years.

    A: What kinds of cars can you fix?

    B: All kinds of cars, both American and foreign.

    A: Mr. Mendoza, can you fix buses, too?

    B: Buses? No, I've never worked on a bus, but I'm sure I can learn.

    A: It's not really a problem. There is a bus company that needs a mechanic, but there are also two car shops that need mechanics. Let me give you their job applications.

    B: Great. Thank you.

2. A: Hello, Mr. Miller. I'm Richard Chu. Welcome to Ready Employment Agency. How can I help you?

    B: Good morning, Mr. Chu. I'm looking for a job.

    A: OK. What experience do you have?

    B: I was a cook for ten years.

    A: Ten years. That's a lot of experience. Were you a cook in a large restaurant?

    B: Yes. I've worked in a large hotel restaurant for the last three years.

    A: Well, Mr. Miller, I'm sure I can help you find a job. I know a local hotel that needs a dinner cook. They also need someone to bake cakes. Do you bake?

    B: Yes, but not very well. I don't have any experience baking cakes.

    A: OK. Then let me give you the application for the cook's position and we'll see what happens.

B: Thank you.

3. A: Good morning. I have an appointment to look for a job through the agency. Are you Ms. Santos?

B: Yes. I'm Miriam Santos. What's your name, please?

A: Christine Powell.

B: Oh, yes, Ms. Powell. What kind of job are you looking for?

A: Well, I was a cab driver before. But there's not enough business here. I'd like another job that pays a little more.

B: You can drive a cab. That's good. How about trucks or buses?

A: I can drive a bus. I have a license for that. I can't drive a truck, though.

B: OK. I have an opening for a bus driver. Would you be interested? It's with a very nice company.

A: Yes, I would.

Listen again. What can they do now? Circle the skills in column B. [Play the tape or read the transcript of Exercise A aloud again.]

Exercise B.
Soo-ha Lee is calling about a job. Look and listen. Read the questions. Circle the answers.

A: Green Garden Company. May I help you?

B: Yes. I'm calling about the gardener's job in the newspaper. My name is Soo-ha Lee.

A: Hello, Ms. Lee. My name is Lilia Silverman. I'm going to ask you some questions, get a little information, and then have someone call you back. Is that OK with you?

B: OK.

A: First, please spell your name for me.

B: It's Soo-ha, S-O-O, hyphen, H-A. Lee, L-E-E.

A: Thank you. Now, do you have any experience?

B: Yes. I was a gardener for a company that takes care of gardens for large apartment buildings and houses.

A: Oh, for how long?

B: Three months. It was a summer job. And I have some experience in my own garden, too. I grow a lot of my own plants.

A: Oh, I'll write all that down. Can you take care of trees?

B: Well, I didn't do that at my last job. But I'm sure I can learn.

A: OK, Ms. Lee. The only other thing I need for now is your phone number.

B: It's 555-2133.

A: 555-2133. OK, thank you. Someone will call you soon.

B: Thank you very much.

Unit 10

Listening (Page 132)
Exercise A.
Look and listen. Write the bus number on the bus.

1. A: I want to go to the mall. Which bus do I take?

B: Take number 8.

A: Which bus?

B: 8. It goes to the mall. It's leaving in fifteen minutes.

A: OK. How much is the fare?

B: $1.00.

A: $1.00, OK. Thanks!

B: You're welcome.

2. A: Excuse me. Does this bus go to Park Street?

B: No, it doesn't. Bus 27 goes to Park Street. You can get the 27 across the street.

A: Do you know the fare?

B: $1.75.

A: Does the $1.75 need to be exact change?

B: Yes, it does.

3. A: I'm going downtown. Which bus do I take?

B: Number 45.

A: Excuse me?

B: Bus 45 goes downtown.

A: Oh, OK. Where can I get it?

B: Right here. It should be here in about ten minutes.

A: Great. Do you know if the fare's still $1.50?

B: Yes. From here to downtown is $1.50.

A: $1.50? Thanks for your help.

B: You're welcome.

Listen again. Match the destination to the correct bus. Write the letter on the bus. *[Play the tape or read the transcript of Exercise A aloud again.]*

Listen again. Write the fares on the signs. *[Play the tape or read the transcript of Exercise A aloud again.]*

Check Your Competency (Page 141)
Exercise D.
Use competency 4. Write the bus numbers in column A.

1. A: Excuse me. Does this bus go to City Hospital?

   B: No, it doesn't. You have to take bus 25.

   A: Which bus?

   B: 25.

   A: How much is the fare?

   B: $1.00.

   A: Only $1.00? Great. Thanks.

2. A: I'm going to City Park. Which bus do I take?

   B: Take bus 7.

   A: How much is the fare for bus 7?

   B: $1.75.

   A: Excuse me? How much?

   B: $1.75.

   A: OK, thanks.

3. A: I want to go to City Adult School. Which bus do I take?

   B: Take bus 16.

   A: How much is the fare for bus 16?

   B: $1.00.

   A: The fare's $1.00?

   B: That's right.

   A: Thank you.

Listen again. Write the fares in column B.

[Play the tape or read the transcript of Exercise A aloud again.]